TRISTAN and ISOLDE

RICHARD WAGNER

TRISTAN and ISOLDE

TRANSLATED AND WITH AN INTRODUCTION BY
STEWART ROBB

A Dutton  *Paperback*

NEW YORK
E. P. DUTTON

This paperback edition of

"Tristan and Isolde"

First published 1965 by E. P. Dutton & Co., Inc.

All rights reserved. Printed in the U.S.A.

Copyright, ©, 1965, by Stewart Robb

SBN 0-525-47173-1

THIS TRANSLATION
IS DEDICATED TO MY DARLING DAUGHTER,
Denise Maurine Munro Robb

Introduction

I. *The Troubles of* Tristan

Shortly after he had completed *Tristan and Isolde* and before he had sent it to Breitkopf & Härtel, Wagner had a premonition. He mentioned it in a letter to Mathilde Wesendonck, written in August, 1860:

> Upon reading it through again, I couldn't believe my eyes or my ears. How terribly I shall have to pay for this work some day, if I intend to see it performed! I distinctly foresee the most unheard-of sufferings; for in it—I can't hide the fact—I've overstepped whatever lies within the powers of execution. Supremely talented performers are the only ones equal to the task; but they are not easily to be found in the world. Yet I cannot resist the temptation, if only to hear the orchestra!

The following year the Grand Ducal Theatre at Karlsruhe accepted *Tristan* for performance and plunged into the rehearsals with genuine enthusiasm. But soon the opera was dropped, for both the singers and orchestra agreed that the work was much too difficult. In 1862 it was picked up by the Vienna Court Opera House with the same enthusiasm that the Karlsruhe Theatre had initially shown. The leading tenor, Aloys Ander, who had been a superb Lohengrin, tackled the part lovingly, but soon he became terrified of it and backed out. There may have been as many as seventy-seven rehearsals, counting the short as well as the long; then in 1863 the work was given up as unsingable.

Wagner's enemies jeered, and the press made merry. One Berlin paper stated pontifically:

> The chief event in our musical life is the laying-aside of Richard Wagner's *Tristan and Isolde* as unproduceable. It

had to come to this: now at last the title of "music of the future," about which there has been so much fighting, is justified: the present cannot even perform this music! . . .

When, thanks to the munificence of King Ludwig II of Bavaria, this glorious opera finally achieved its world première in Munich in 1865, the three performances, though superb and successful, were preceded, attended, and followed by so many disasters that Wagner was proved a sure prophet.

One of the first of these disasters occurred when Hans von Bülow, Wagner's good friend and disciple who was scheduled to conduct the première, was told that to extend the area for the orchestra would require the sacrifice of thirty stalls. He shouted: "What does it matter whether we have thirty *Schweinehunde* more or less in the place?" That finished him. The Munich press raged against him furiously for an entire week and never, indeed, actually let up on "the insolent Prussian" until he decided to flee the city, which he did soon after the third performance.

Wagner, who was basking in King Ludwig's favor, was quickly becoming the *bête-noire* of the courtiers, hangers-on, and politicians of Munich when they discovered to their chagrin that he was no easy road to Ludwig's ear and influence. On the contrary, so utterly uncorruptible was the composer that his enemies began to consider him all kinds of evil things: republican, Communist, free-thinker—something they had suspected all along—and a brutal, vicious press campaign flared up against him, inspired, it is believed, by the cabinet or court, or both. Slander spread like wildfire around the naïve composer. One of these foul rumors—one that still crops up occasionally—even insinuated that the relations between Wagner and Ludwig were immoral.[1]

---

[1] This canard is not accepted by biographers and other historians because there is not an iota of evidence to support it. The letters that passed between the two men expressing undying love might seem like calf love to the average Anglo-Saxon reader, but their fulsomeness is not uncommon to the European, even today. The king, it is now believed, was abnormal, but Ernest Newman presents evidence that the same private diary that proves him to have been so indicates that Wagner was not. After homosexual lapses and struggles against this vice, "it is almost invariably Wagner and his opera texts that Ludwig summons to his aid to steel him in his hard fight." "Wagner never had any leanings

According to Newman, the politicians who attacked Wagner and finally succeeded in driving him from Munich, thereby only making the monarch more withdrawn and unapproachable than ever "were completely lacking in an understanding of a nature like the King's. They should have made use of Wagner as an artist. But for that they were too unsubtle: they made the mistake of trying to use him simply as a politician; and when they realised that he had no intention of being their pawn in mere political intrigues they resolved to destroy him."[2]

At last the day scheduled for the première of *Tristan* arrived. May 15, 1865 began badly, even catastrophically. In the early morning bailiffs invaded Wagner's home at Briennerstrasse 21, for an old, heavy, and unexpected debt had caught up with the composer. A provisional distraint was levied on his furniture. But Cosima ran frantically to King Ludwig's treasury, which promptly paid the bill of 2,400 florins.

Scarcely had that crisis passed when another and worse one developed. News was brought to Wagner that Malvina Schnorr, who was to perform the part of Isolde, had developed such hoarseness in her voice that she could not sing that night. Wagner enthusiasts, including many important people from all over Europe and beyond had arrived for this première, which now had to be canceled and rescheduled for June 10th.

The performance itself, which finally took place on the new date, was a triumph, and Wagner was elated. Two more equally fine performances followed. Then came a real disaster. Ludwig Schnorr, who was not only the first Tristan but probably the greatest of all Tristans in opera history, died suddenly. The death-bed scene was highly melodramatic. In almost his last paroxysms he sang passages from Siegfried, then cried, "I must see you once more! Richard, do you not hear me?" Wagner was heartbroken over the loss of his irre-

---

whatever in that direction. For this gossip there was never the slightest foundation in fact. Among the documents preserved in the Wahnfried archives, indeed, is a jotting of his of 1873 in which he notes that 'there is one thing about the Greeks that we shall never be able to understand, a thing which separates them utterly from us: their love—pederasty.' " *The Life of Richard Wagner* (New York: Alfred A. Knopf, 1948), Vol. III, pp. 244, 237.

[2] *Ibid.*, p. 252, footnote.

placeable tenor and mourned: "Mein Trauter! Mein Trauter! For me he lived, for me he died!"

Schnorr's death led to more trouble, and of a strange kind. The grieving widow, Wagner's Isolde, promptly got in touch with a medium through whom she soon believed she was in contact with her husband. The husband—or whatever—announced to Frau Schnorr that henceforth her mission in life should be to play a guiding part in Wagner's career. Elliott Zuckerman writes: "This 'mission' would justify her husband's self-sacrifice for the Wagnerian cause. *Tristan* as much as spiritualism determined the nature of Malvina's delusions. She and Wagner were to effect a Platonic union of souls: he would find redemption through the love of the 'pure divine womanliness' he had so often celebrated in his works. She idealized herself just as Wagner had idealized Mathilde Wesendonck a decade earlier: Tristanizing had returned to plague its inventor."[3]

Frau Schnorr kept her medium by her so as to be in constant touch with her dear departed. She also wrote messages to him which were answered in her dreams. The reiterated urgings from the spirit-world were apparently that Frau Schnorr should take up the reins in Wagner's life and that he should influence King Ludwig to marry her. The composer was horrified at this unremitting pestering by "the crazy woman," the more so when the determined widow, after casting baleful eyes on Cosima von Bülow, threatened to expose to the king and court and the world at large the fact that Wagner and Von Bülow's wife were living in sin. Finally, however, the tempest blew over.

How true had Wagner's prediction become!

II. *The Meaning of* Tristan

The key word to an understanding of the philosophy of *Tristan and Isolde* is *Liebestod*.

Liebestod means love-death, death-in-love, love-in-death, love's death, a love satisfied and consummated only by death. Now break the word into its components, taking *Liebe* ("love") first. To Richard Wagner, love between man and

[3] *The First Hundred Years of Wagner's Tristan* (New York and London, 1964), pp. 58-59.

woman is an insatiable desire. He knew, for he had powerful sex urges that he deplored, but often satisfied. But he was also aware of higher forms of love. He once wrote to his niece Johanna: "My one need is love! Fame, honor—nothing of that kind can refresh me: only one thing can delight me and reconcile me to life—a sign that I am loved, even if it comes only from a child!" Spiritual love and purity he knew too, and later he would give these their full artistic expression in *Parsifal*.

To Liszt, in a letter dated December 16, 1854, he wrote: "As I have never in life felt the real bliss of my love, I must erect a monument to the most beautiful of all my dreams, in which, from beginning to end, that love shall be thoroughly satiated. I have in my head *Tristan and Isolde*, the simplest but most full-blooded musical conception . . ."

Today, if a person of culture is asked what the world's two greatest monuments to love are, will he not reply, "Shakespeare's *Romeo and Juliet* and Wagner's *Tristan and Isolde*"?

The other component of *Liebestod* is *Tod*, "death." During this period of Wagner's career the word *Tod* to him meant nothingness, the termination of the evils of life. This is evident in another passage from the same letter to Liszt quoted above:

> I have of late occupied myself exclusively with a man who has come like a gift from heaven, although only a literary one, into my solitude. This is Arthur Schopenhauer, the greatest philosopher since Kant, whose thoughts, as he himself expresses it, he has thought out to the end. . . . His chief idea, the final negation of the desire of life, is terribly serious, but it shows the only salvation possible. To me of course that thought was not new, and it can indeed be conceived by no one in whom it did not pre-exist, but this philosopher was the first to place it clearly before me. If I think of the storm of my heart, the terrible tenacity with which it used to cling to the hope of life, and if even now I feel this hurricane within me, I have at least found a quietus which in wakeful nights helps me to sleep. This is the genuine, ardent longing for death, for absolute unconsciousness, total non-existence. Freedom from all dreams is our only final salvation.

By the following year Wagner's thoughts had not grown less grim, for in a letter to his friend he speaks of "this terrible world, with an empty nothing beyond it."

As is not the case with the earlier Lohengrin and Tann-
häuser, nowhere in *Tristan and Isolde* do the protagonists in-
voke or even name God, Christ, or the Holy Mother, although
the story is set in the devoutly Catholic Arthurian period. And
the philosophy of the two lovers is the same as that of Wagner
at this time. They long rhapsodically for death as the only
possible quietus for their unquenchable longing for each other.
For instance, when the mortally wounded Tristan briefly re-
covers from his coma-like state at the beginning of Act III, he
describes death in these words:

> Yet where I tarried
> I cannot really tell you.
> The sun I did not see,
> nor saw I land and people:
> yet, what I saw,
> I can indeed not tell you.
> I was
> where I have been forever,
> where I forever go:
> the realm of night
> which girds the world.
> We have there one knowledge only:
> godlike, endless
> prime oblivion!

Yet the poet-musician, like his idol Schopenhauer, was ever
the moralist. Therefore, even in *Tristan and Isolde* he cannot
avoid adding a touch of mysticism to the bleak concept of
death as "prime oblivion." Thus are allayed the horror and
amorality of the thought that the ultimate goal allotted to both
saint and sinner is identical. This should not be, and both
Wagner and Schopenhauer knew it should not be. In Schopenhauer, for instance, after we learn that the truly wise man will
renounce life and its phantasms, we are given an answer to
the question that asks how such a wise man is better off
than the hedonist. Is their end not the same? No, says the
pessimist-philosopher. If the human consciousness dies without
having properly learned its lesson of utter detachment from
material existence by negation of the will-to-live, that life
force will be punished by manifesting itself again in some
form of earthly existence. A form of reincarnation, if one
wishes to call it so. But for him who has renounced with his

entire being the baubles of this earth death will bring about a complete end of individual consciousness and what Sir Thomas Browne sarcastically called "ingestion into the divine shadow."

In this philosophy some have seen a resemblance to the Nirvana of Buddhism. Contrasting this concept with that of the Christian heaven, G. K. Chesterton said in serious jest: "The Christian heaven is a heaven where they love one another: the Buddhist heaven is a heaven where they *are* one another." In Wagner's music-drama may be found a mystical mingling of both concepts:

TRISTAN: But should we die,
we would not part,
joined forever,
without end,
never waking,
never fearing,
nameless there,
in love enfolded,
each to each belonging,
with love alone our life source!
* * *

BOTH: Noble surcease . . .
. . . no more sundered,
yet alone . . .
ISOLDE: You Isolde . . .
TRISTAN: . . . you Tristan!
ISOLDE: Tristan I . . .
TRISTAN: . . . I Isolde!
ISOLDE: No more Isolde!
TRISTAN: No more Tristan!
BOTH: No more naming . . .
both one mind . . .

And in the last scene of all, when Isolde dies, she expects to be lost with her lover

in the World Spirit's
infinite All,
to drown now,
descending,
void of thought—
highest bliss!

But then, thought Wagner, as did Hamlet, there's a rub. Is death pure nothingness, or does it harbor within its precincts some strange state of awareness? By 1860 Wagner had written his essay, "Prelude to *Tristan and Isolde*," in which this doubt is expressed:

> It is the bliss of quitting life, of being no more, of last redemption into that wondrous realm from which we stray the furthest when we strive to enter it by fiercest force. Shall we call it death? Or is it not night's wonder world, whence —as the story says—an ivy and a vine sprang up in locked embrace over Tristan and Isolde's grave?

The same thought is to be found in his love-drama. Says Tristan:

> It is the dark
> nocturnal land
> from whence my mother
> sent me forth
> when, in the throes of
> death they bore me;
> in dying
> she gave me daylight's kingdom.
> From the time I was born
> her loving refuge was
> the wonder-realm of night,
> from where I woke to light.

This poetic but gloomy Tristanizing philosophy lived in Wagner's mind until April 29, 1864, when a miracle occurred that swept away the negative part of it forevermore. In fact, all that remained of the *Tristan* philosophy was the duty of renunciation, which is a recurring theme through all of Wagner's works.

Wagner's position early in 1864 was desperate. Writes his biographer, Ernest Newman:

> After the fiasco of the *Tristan* rehearsals in Vienna it was unlikely that any other theatre would take up that seemingly impossible work, while belief in the ultimate impracticability of the still unfinished *Ring* was by now fairly general, even among his friends and well-wishers. His debts were by this

time colossal for a man in his circumstances; and after the publicity given to them by his flight from Vienna it was unlikely that he would enjoy much credit anywhere in the future. Vienna itself, as a place of residence, was henceforth closed to him; and the Vienna Opera happened to be, after Berlin, the most important institution of its kind in the German-speaking countries. Most of his friends, especially those who had any money, were tired of him and a little afraid of him. . . . He was within a few weeks of his fifty-first birthday, without much prospect of income except by concert conducting, which repelled and exhausted him. He had in a drawer, precisely as in 1860, three complete new works and two-thirds of a fourth, with no apparent possibility of the production of any of them. From whatever point of view he looked at his life, it must have seemed a complete and irrevocable failure.[4]

His mental state was in utter turmoil. One may imagine how he felt when even a few years earlier he was able to write: "Everything I do fills me with disgust. It can't go on forever. I can't stand such a life any longer. I will kill myself rather than live like this. . . . I don't believe in anything . . ."

He had enough wry humor left in him, however, to write this epitaph for himself:

> Here lies Wagner, who never amounted to much, was not even knighted, never achieved anything, not even a degree from a university.

When about to depart for Stuttgart, where he planned to hide from his creditors, he said to Frau Wille, "My friend, you do not know how great my suffering is, nor the depths of the misery that lies before me." She replied comfortingly, in what appears to have been a premonition of good: "O! not misery! Something will happen. I do not know what, but it will be something good, something different from what you think. Have patience: good fortune will come."[5]

---

[4] *The Life of Richard Wagner,* Vol. III, pp. 210-211.

[5] *Ibid.,* p. 218, footnote. Wagner himself seems to have once had a premonition of good. In a letter to Mathilde Wesendonck dated May 2, 1860, he writes: "I shall leave it also to my protecting daemon to summon the man who shall one day reveal these (final) works of mine to the world."

Then came the miracle. Wagner's epic poem, *The Ring of the Nibelung,* issued in 1863, had fallen into the hands of an unknown admirer of Wagner, the young Crown Prince Ludwig of Bavaria. In his "Preface to The King," Wagner, enlarging upon how hopeless it would be to try to get an adequate performance of *The Ring* under the ordinary conditions of the German theatre of the day, admitted that it could nevertheless be done through the cooperation of a number of German art-lovers or through the help of a German prince. "Will this Prince be found?" were Wagner's final words: "In the beginning was the Deed!"

Less than a year later, in March 1864, the prince found himself king, legally of full age (18), and with the forces of the Royal Treasury at his disposal to carry out his ideals.

The rest is well-known history. One of the first acts of the young king was to order that Wagner be sought out and brought to him. On April 29th the despondent musician was finally found hiding from creditors in Stuttgart. The Cabinet Secretary announced himself, told him he had instructions to take him back at once to Munich, and handed him a photograph of the king and a ring. Everything the composer needed, Pfistermeister stated, would be at his disposal in Munich, and *Tristan* and *The Ring* would be produced there. He was told to prepare to leave for Munich the next day. On the morning of that day Wagner wrote gratefully to the king:

> These tears of the heavenliest emotion I send to you, to tell you that now the marvels of poetry have come as a divine reality into my poor, love-lacking life. And that life, its last poetry, its last tones, belong henceforth to you, my gracious young King: dispose of them as your own property.

And the king kept the promises that he made to Wagner in a letter of May 5th:

> Rest assured that I will do everything in my power to make up to you for what you have suffered in the past. The mean cares of everyday life I will banish from you forever; I will produce for you the peace you have longed for in order that you may be free to spread the mighty wings of your genius in the pure aether of rapturous art. Though you were unconscious of it, you were *the sole source of my de-*

light from my tenderest youth onwards, my friend who
spoke to my heart as no other did, my best teacher and
educator. I will repay you everything to the best of my
ability. O how I have looked forward to the time when I
could do this! I hardly dared indulge myself in the hope so
soon to be able to prove my love to you.

Wagner had once been deeply stirred by reading the biography of a hero of antiquity. He wrote, in a letter to Malwida
von Meysenbug: "I have, by chance, just been reading
Plutarch's life of Timoleon. That life ended very happily—a
rare and unheard-of thing, especially in history. It does one
good to think that such a thing is possible. It moved me
profoundly."

And now, thanks to a wonderful happening, Wagner's later
career was to have a happy ending, as equally rare and
unheard-of as that of Timoleon, yet as much a fact of history.
True, there were storms and upsets to come, but when Wagner
passed away nineteen years later, it was as one blessed by
God.

No wonder that when his friend Franz Liszt heard the good
news he wrote exultantly in a letter to the Princess Wittgen-
stein: "As for Wagner's position, it savours of the prodigious.
Solomon was wrong: there *is* something new under the sun!"[6]

Scarcely had the composer become sumptuously installed in
his new home in Munich than a woman with a claim to clair-
voyance, Frau Dangl, called on him to talk about himself and
the king. "According to her, the two previous kings of Bavaria
had done themselves no good by failing to follow her advice."
"Do you believe in the stars? It is written in them that this
young king is called to great deeds. I want him to have peace,
and you, Herr Wagner, must guard him against the machina-
tions of evil men who would ruin him as they ruined his
father and grandfather." Powerfully impressed, Wagner wrote
to Mathilde Maier the next day:

The fate of this wonderful, unique youth, who is profoundly linked with me by a mystical magic is entrusted to
me, *me*. There is a lofty, marvellous significance in his love.
To abandon him to the scum of intrigue and corruption

[6] *Ibid.*, p. 268.

would be a treachery against the reproach of which I would have no defence. The profound meaning of my duty to the King, which is of significance to a whole people, nay, to Germany itself, has been revealed to me through an almost supernatural experience. I ask myself now, "Why this cup to *my* lips? I, who want only peace, peace, liberty to belong to myself. I to hold in my hands the destiny of a nation, of a glorious indescribably endowed King![7]

Wagner's faith in his destiny had come back to him a thousand-fold. It may be stated that from that happy day of April 29, 1864 the composer felt an overwhelming sense of God's presence and care that never thereafter left him. Once (in 1874) when Cosima remarked to him: "In spite of all I feel that God loves us and is protecting us," he replied: "Yes, indeed, the whole world is blind, but nonetheless bears within it an impulse towards truth and realization. Every good thing that has been, still exists, one has only to disregard space and time, for eternity is present in every moment. The whole is for ever reproducing itself over and over again. If there is light it cannot be extinguished, it must illuminate."

One thing was certain. Gone now for good was the Schopenhauer-Buddhistic philosophy of despair so fundamental to *Tristan*. Instead there was now Providence, God, and His Christ. God must be in His heaven indeed, for here was palpable proof that He takes care of those who have a message from God to the world. Now Wagner could say with Longfellow, "Life is real, life is earnest: and the grave is not the goal."

The composer felt profoundly grateful to the Lord in heaven as well as to his lord on earth. Romain Rolland relates that a friend visiting Wagner in his latter, halcyon days, noticed that the composer said grace before meat, and asked why. "Because I believe in my Saviour," said Wagner simply. His writings from this post-*Tristan* period bear out this fact. They are so devoutly and even profoundly Christian that it is surprising that Nietzsche the anti-Christ had to wait for *Parsifal* to appear before becoming alienated from the Master of Bayreuth.

Wagner's letters took on a particularly religious fervency.

[7] *Ibid.,* pp. 359-360.

For instance, in writing to his good Jewish friend[8] Angelo Neumann, to whom he had given complete legal production rights to all his music-dramas, Wagner said: "This will take not only all your energy and capacities, but also a firm trust in the Lord—and that I feel you have. So may heaven bless you and all dependent upon you, and keep you in its sheltering care." Statements like these were now typical of the new Wagner.

Wagner had acquired an unshakable faith in the power of prayer, and in his overwhelming gratitude to his princely pro-

---

[8] A Jewish friend? Yes, he had many among his best friends. They had read his *Judaism in Music* (mild stuff today) and had not been fazed by it. Wagner was pro-Jewish in practice, anti-Jewish only in words, and not always then. When he wanted his most German of operas, *Die Meistersinger,* arranged for piano, he gave the job to his Jewish friend Carl Tausig. When he wanted his "most Christian of works," *Parsifal,* to be superbly conducted, he gave the baton to another of his good Jewish friends, Hermann Levi, son of a rabbi. When he invited a musician to live with him and his family at Wahnfried, the one so favored was a Jew, Joseph Rubinstein. He was also assigned to do the piano part of *Parsifal.* Nor would Wagner have anything to do with organized anti-Semitism. When approached by a rabid anti-Semitic organization to sign a petition against the Jews, Wagner was shocked and would have nothing to do with it. Hermann Levi wrote to his father: "He really is the best and most honorable of men: even his fight against what he calls Judaism in music is sustained by the loftiest motives. His attitude to me, to Rubinstein, and to Tausig shows that he harbors none of the petty prejudices that Junker land-owners or bigoted Protestants do."

Wagner's pro-Jewish practices grew to such a pitch that the frequently hostile German press began to call Wagner himself a Jew. They referred to him as "the Rabbi of Bayreuth." The German caricaturists began to give a Jewish turn to his features. In the Vienna *Floh* of 1879 a cartoon shows him surrounded by Jewish children and looking exaggeratedly Jewish himself. A drawing in the Vienna *Kikeriki* of 1882 shows an audience of Jews applauding *Parsifal.* Accompanying the cartoon are these words: "Wagner has become the God of the Jews, to whom they pour out their adoration." About 1880 a satirical novel appeared, *Verliebte Wagnerianer,* in which Wagner figures as the composer Goldschein. Nietzsche's rumors that Wagner had had a Jewish father, had done their work. The rumor was not scotched till Otto Bournot did his researches.

tector and supporter he vowed that if ever the Wagner theatre
and its *Ring* production became a reality he would match "so
great a prize" with "a great oblation" on his part: he would
"remain far from the Festival, deny myself the prodigious
effect of the dedication, but humbly pay homage in secret
prayer to my good genius, my godlike Friend and Fulfiller.
Such was my oath. Shall I live to have to keep it?" He did, as
is proved by an entry in the privacy of his diary, under date
of 1st January, 1867: "Zurich . . . Theatre model—Homeward
journey: Vow."

Prayer had healing power, the post-*Tristan* Wagner believed. In 1878 he spoke of a breviary that arrested his atten-
tion: "It tells how, as much through the merit of Jesus Christ
as by their medical skill, Cosmas and his brother Damian,
two famous physicians from Arabia healed diseases which
had been considered incurable." His wife Cosima, he was
convinced, had healing hands.

No longer did he believe that death is "prime oblivion,"
"empty nothing," or "total non-existence." Man, Wagner was
now sure, is an immortal being, not bound by or subject to
the time and space of mortal existence. His first definite asser-
tion of man's immortality can be found in his *On State and
Religion*, written shortly after his rescue from despair, in the
winter of 1864-1865:

> To the religious eye the truth grows plain that there must
> be another world than this, because the inextinguishable
> bent to happiness cannot be stilled within this world, and
> hence requires another world for its redemption.

This other world is spiritual and can be seen only with the
awakened spiritual senses:

> What, now, is that other world? So far as the conceptual
> faculties of human understanding reach, and in their prac-
> tical application as intellectual reason, it is quite impossible
> to gain a notion that shall not clearly show itself as founded
> on this selfsame world of need and change: wherefore, since
> this world is the source of our unhappiness, that other
> world, of redemption from it, must be precisely as different
> from this present world as the mode of cognizance whereby
> we are to perceive that other world must be different from

the mode which shows us nothing but this present world of suffering and illusion.

One time, as we read in Du Moulin-Eckert's biography of Cosima Wagner, the composer was reading aloud from Danner's book of ghost stories. Cosima wrote, "We were deeply agitated. 'The important question is whether we are in communion with the spirits of those dear to us,' said Richard, who has a great leaning toward those realms, and perhaps, unconsciously a great connexion with them." "Death alone was a grave matter, as a test of life," he said at another time, "but all that came after it was as kindly as possible. Though, thank God, a deep mystery still lies over it all." This last statement seems to indicate that Wagner, though he may have believed communication possible, held the orthodox Christian's distaste for anything that might savor of spiritualism.

Thus Wagner learned that the one and only possible answer to the world's suffering was Jesus Christ the Redeemer. And to follow him, believing in His blood, is to abandon forever nationalism, patriotism, and racism. Wagner said:

> Jesus teaches us to break through the barriers of patriotism and find out our amplest satisfaction in the weal of all the human race.
>
> *   *   *
>
> The blood of the Saviour, the issue from his head, his wounds upon the cross—who impiously would ask its race, if white or otherwise? Divine we call it, and its source that Godlike pity which streams through all the human species, its fount and origin.
>
> *   *   *
>
> The blood of suffering mankind, as sublimated in that wondrous birth, could never flow in the interest of howsoever favored a single race; no, it sheds itself on all the human family, for noblest cleansing of man's blood from every stain. Hence the sublime simplicity of the pure Christian religion, whereas the Brahminic, for instance, applying its knowledge of the world to the insurance of supremacy for one advantaged race, became lost . . . and sank to the extreme of the absurd. Thus, notwithstanding that we have seen the blood of noblest races vitiated by admixture, the partaking of the blood of Jesus, as symbolized in the only

genuine sacrament of the Christian religion, might raise the very lowest races to the purity of gods. This would have been the antidote to the decline of races through commingling, and perhaps our earthball brought forth breathing life for no other purpose than that ministrance of healing.

Friedrich Nietzsche, the most notorious anti-Christ of the nineteenth century, who had first been attracted to Wagner through the music-drama *Tristan*, was now disgusted. "Richard Wagner," he exclaimed, "apparently the most complete of victors, has fallen suddenly, helpless and broken, before the Christian cross!"

Yes; the creator of *Tristan and Isolde* had become the creator of *Parsifal*.

STEWART ROBB

New York City
1965

TRISTAN and ISOLDE

CHARACTERS

TRISTAN, *a world-renowned hero and nephew of King Mark*

KING MARK, *the ruler of Cornwall*

ISOLDE, *an Irish princess*

KURVENAL, *Tristan's faithful friend*

MELOT, *false friend to Tristan*

BRANGAENE, *Isolde's maidservant*

A SHEPHERD

A HELMSMAN

SAILORS, KNIGHTS, *and* ATTENDANTS

SCENE OF ACTION

ACT I.   At sea on the deck of Tristan's ship, on the voyage
from Ireland to Cornwall.

ACT II. King Mark's castle in Cornwall.

ACT III. Tristan's castle in Brittany.

ERSTER AUFZUG

Zeltartiges Gemach auf dem Vorderdeck eines Seeschiffes, reich mit Teppichen behangen, beim Beginn nach dem Hintergrunde zu gänzlich geschlossen; zur Seite führt eine schmale Treppe in den Schiffsraum hinab. — Isolde auf einem Ruhebett, das Gesicht in die Kissen gedrückt. Brangäne, einen Teppich zurückgeschlagen haltend, blickt zur Seite über Bord.

ERSTER AUFTRITT

Isolde. Brangäne. Stimme eines jungen Seemanns.

STIMME EINES JUNGEN SEEMANNS *(aus der Höhe, wie vom Mast her, vernehmbar):*
>Westwärts
>schweift der Blick:
>ostwärts
>streicht das Schiff.
>Frisch weht der Wind
>der Heimat zu:
>mein irisch Kind,
>wo weilest du?
>Sind's deiner Seufzer Wehen,
>die mir die Segel blähen?
>Wehe, wehe, du Wind!
>Weh, ach wehe, mein Kind!
>Irische Maid,
>du wilde, minnige Maid!

ISOLDE *(jäh auffahrend):*
>Wer wagt mich zu höhnen?
>*(Sie blickt verstört um sich.)*
>Brangäne, du?
>Sag — wo sind wir?

A C T I

SCENE I

A pavilion, richly hung with rugs, on the forward deck of a sailing ship, at first entirely closed at the back; on one side a narrow hatchway leads to the cabin below.

Isolde on a couch, her face buried in the cushions. Brangaene, her maidservant, holding back a curtain, looks out over the side of the ship.

THE VOICE OF A YOUNG SAILOR *(from above, as if from the masthead)*:

> Westward
> roams my gaze:
> eastward
> plies the ship.
> The wind blows fresh
> toward land of home:
> my Irish child,
> where do you roam?
> Is it your windy sighing
> that keeps my vessel flying?
> Breezes, blow; breezes, blow!
> Child, they bring only woe!
> My Irish maid,
> you wild, lovable maid!

ISOLDE *(starting up, and looking around, disturbed)*:

> Who here dares to mock me?
> Brangaene, ho!
> Say—where are we?

BRANGÄNE *(an der Öffnung)*:

Blaue Streifen
stiegen im Westen auf;
sanft und schnell
segelt das Schiff:
auf ruhiger See vor Abend
erreichen wir sicher das Land.

ISOLDE: Welches Land?

BRANGÄNE: Kornwalls grünen Strand.

ISOLDE: Nimmermehr!
                 Nicht heut noch morgen!

BRANGÄNE *(läßt den Vorhang zufallen und eilt bestürzt zu Isolde)*:

Was hör' ich? Herrin! Ha!

ISOLDE *(wild vor sich hin)*:

Entartet Geschlecht!
Unwert der Ahnen!
Wohin, Mutter,
vergabst du die Macht,
über Meer und Sturm zu gebieten?
O zahme Kunst
der Zauberin,
die nur Balsamtränke noch braut!
Erwache mir wieder,
kühne Gewalt;
herauf aus dem Busen,
wo du dich bargst!
Hört meinen Willen,
zagende Winde!
Heran zu Kampf
und Wettergetös'!
Zu tobender Stürme
wütendem Wirbel!
Treibt aus dem Schlaf
dies träumende Meer,
weckt aus dem Grund
seine grollende Gier!
Zeigt ihm die Beute,
die ich ihm biete!

BRANGAENE *(at the opening)*:
> Blue the streaks
> that rise from the western sky;
> soft and swift,
> onward we sail;
> a sea that is calm will bring us
> quite safely to land ere it's dark.

ISOLDE: What land?

BRANGAENE: Cornwall's grassy shore.

ISOLDE:
> Nevermore,
> today or ever!

BRANGAENE *(lets fall the curtain and hastens anxiously to Isolde)*:
> What say you? Mistress! Ha!

ISOLDE *(with wild gaze)*:
> Degenerate stock!
> Shame of your forebears!
> Where now, Mother,
> have you given your power
> to command the sea and the tempest?
> O feeble art
> of sorceress,
> that now only brews balsam drink!
> Bold spirit of mast'ry,
> rouse me again;
> come out from that bosom
> wherein you hide!
> Hear, trembling winds,
> the orders I give you!
> To arms, to breast
> the elements' roar
> and blustering tempest's
> furious vortex!
> Drive from its sleep
> this slumbering sea,
> stir up the deep
> till it growls in its greed!
> Show it the booty
> which I now offer!

Zerschlag es dies trotzige Schiff,
des zerschellten Trümmer verschling's!
Und was auf ihm lebt,
den wehenden Atem,
den laß ich euch Winden zum Lohn!

BRANGÄNE *(im äußersten Schreck, um Isolde sich bemühend)*:
O weh!
Ach! Ach
des Übels, das ich geahnt!
Isolde! Herrin!
Teures Herz!
Was bargst du mir so lang?
Nicht eine Träne
weintest du Vater und Mutter;
kaum einen Gruß
den Bleibenden botest du.
Von der Heimat scheidend
kalt und stumm,
bleich und schweigend
auf der Fahrt;
ohne Nahrung,
ohne Schlaf;
starr und elend,
wild verstört:
wie ertrug ich,
so dich sehend,
nichts dir mehr zu sein,
fremd vor dir zu stehn?
O, nun melde,
was dich müht!
Sage, künde,
was dich quält!
Herrin Isolde,
trauteste Holde!
Soll sie wert sich dir wähnen,
vertraue nun Brangänen!

ISOLDE: Luft! Luft!
Mir erstickt das Herz!
Öffne! Öffne dort weit!
*(Brangäne zieht eilig die Vorhänge in der
Mitte auseinander.)*

> Demolish this insolent ship,
> let it break and shiver to bits!
> And all that survives,
> as flickering spirits,
> I leave to you winds for your pay!

BRANGAENE (*in alarm and concern for Isolde*):
> O woe!
> Ah! Ah!
> The ill I feared has arrived!
> Isolde! Mistress!
> Dearest heart!
> What have you hid so long?
> You did not shed
> one tear for your father and mother;
> you scarcely bade
> farewell to those left behind,
> and with stony coldness
> left your home,
> pale and silent
> all the trip;
> food you took not,
> nor did sleep,
> numb and wretched,
> wild, distraught:
> how could I endure
> to see this?
> Am I nothing now,
> nothing but a stone?
> Just what was it
> tired you so?
> Tell me plainly
> what torments.
> Lady Isolde,
> dearly beloved one,
> if you think she is worthy,
> then you should trust Brangaene.

ISOLDE:
> Air! Air!
> Oh, my heart constricts!
> Open, open there wide!

Brangaene hastily draws apart the curtains in the center.

ZWEITER AUFTRITT

Die Vorigen. Tristan. Kurwenal. Schiffsvolk, Ritter und Knappen.

(Man blickt dem Schiff entlang bis zum Steuerbord, über den Bord hinaus auf das Meer und den Horizont. Um den Hauptmast in der Mitte ist Seevolk, mit Tauen beschäftigt, gelagert; über sie hinaus gewahrt man am Steuerbord Ritter und Knappen, ebenfalls gelagert; von ihnen etwas entfernt Tristan, mit verschränkten Armen stehend und sinnend in das Meer blickend; zu Füßen ihm, nachlässig gelagert, Kurwenal.)

STIMME DES JUNGEN SEEMANNS *(vom Maste her, aus der Höhe)*:

> Frisch weht der Wind
> der Heimat zu:
> mein irisch Kind,
> wo weilest du?
> Sind's deiner Seufzer Wehen,
> die mir die Segel blähen?
> Wehe, wehe, du Wind!
> Weh, ach wehe, mein Kind!

ISOLDE *(deren Blick sogleich Tristan fand und starr auf ihn geheftet blieb, dumpf für sich)*:

> Mir erkoren,
> mir verloren,
> hehr und heil,
> kühn und feig!
> Todgeweihtes Haupt!
> Todgeweihtes Herz!
> *(Zu Brangäne, unheimlich lachend.)*
> Was hältst du von dem Knechte?

BRANGÄNE *(ihrem Blicke folgend)*:

> Wen meinst du?

ISOLDE:

> Dort den Helden,
> der meinem Blick
> den seinen birgt,
> in Scham und Scheue
> abwärts schaut.
> Sag, wie dünkt er dich?

SCENE II

*One can see the whole length of the ship to starboard, with
the sea and the horizon beyond. In the center, above the main-
mast, are sailors, busied with ropes, and lying around; beyond
them, in the stern, are groups of knights and attendants, also
seated; a little apart stands Tristan, his arms folded, gazing
thoughtfully out to sea; at his feet Kurvenal reclines carelessly.
From the masthead above is once more heard the voice of
the young sailor.*

THE VOICE OF THE YOUNG SAILOR:

> The wind blows fresh
> toward land of home:
> my Irish child,
> where do you roam?
> Is it your windy sighing
> that keeps my vessel flying?
> Breezes, blow; breezes, blow!
> Child, they bring only woe!

ISOLDE *(whose eyes have at once sought Tristan and fixed
stonily on him—aside, gloomily)*:

> My elected,
> now the lost one,
> great and strong,
> brave and craven!
> Death-devoted head!
> Death-devoted heart!
> *(To Brangaene, laughing unnaturally.)*
> What think you of that fellow?

BRANGAENE *(following her look)*:

> Whom mean you?

ISOLDE:

> There, the hero,
> who cannot look me
> in the eye,
> but looks away
> in frightened shame.
> Say, what d'you think of him?

BRANGÄNE: Frägst du nach Tristan,
                   teure Frau,
                   dem Wunder aller Reiche,
                   dem hochgepriesnen Mann,
                   dem Helden ohne Gleiche,
                   des Ruhmes Hort und Bann?

ISOLDE *(sie verhöhnend)*:
                   Der zagend vor dem Streiche
                   sich flüchtet, wo er kann,
                   weil eine Braut er als Leiche
                   für seinen Herrn gewann!
                   Dünkt es dich dunkel,
                   mein Gedicht?
                   Frag ihn denn selbst,
                   den freien Mann,
                   ob mir zu nahn er wagt?
                   Der Ehren Gruß
                   und zücht'ge Acht
                   vergißt der Herrin
                   der zage Held,
                   daß ihr Blick ihn nur nicht erreiche,
                   den Helden ohne Gleiche!
                   O, er weiß
                   wohl, warum!
                   Zu dem Stolzen geh,
                   meld ihm der Herrin Wort:
                   Meinem Dienst bereit,
                   schleunig soll er mir nahn.

BRANGÄNE: Soll ich ihn bitten,
                   dich zu grüßen?

ISOLDE: Befehlen ließ
                   dem Eigenholde
                   Furcht der Herrin
                   ich, Isolde!
                   *(Auf Isoldes gebieterischen Wink entfernt
                   sich Brangäne und schreitet verschämt dem
                   Deck entlang dem Steuerbord zu, an den
                   arbeitenden Seeleuten vorbei. Isolde, mit
                   starrem Blicke ihr folgend, zieht sich rück-
                   lings nach dem Ruhebett zurück, wo sie
                   sitzend während des Folgenden bleibt, das
                   Auge unabgewandt nach dem Steuerbord
                   gerichtet.)*

BRANGAENE: Can you mean Tristan,
lady dear,
that marvel of all nations,
that pinnacle of praise,
that hero without equal,
the prize and vaunt of fame?

ISOLDE *(scornfully)*:
Who, trembling at his triumph,
seeks refuge where he can,
fearing to bring to his sov'reign
a corpse instead of a bride.
Think you my saying
is too dark?
Ask him yourself,
that free-born man,
if he will dare come near.
The shrinking hero
has forgot
the forms of greeting
and respect,
for he fears that her glance may reach him,
this hero without equal!
Oh, he knows
well, just why!
To this proud one, go,
bear him his lady's word!
Let him straightway come,
ready for my command.

BRANGAENE: Am I to bid him
offer duty?

ISOLDE: Just let this lord,
so self-sufficient,
fear his mistress,
me, Isolde!

*At a gesture of command from Isolde,
Brangaene leaves her, and timidly makes
her way along the deck, past the busy
sailors, to the stern; Isolde gazes after with
a blank expression, then sinks back on the
couch, where she remains seated during the
following, her eyes still fixed sternward.*

KURWENAL (*der Brangäne kommen sieht, zupft, ohne sich zu erheben, Tristan am Gewande*):

> Hab acht, Tristan!
> Botschaft von Isolde.

TRISTAN (*auffahrend*):

> Was ist? Isolde? —
> (*Er faßt sich schnell, als Brangäne vor ihm anlangt und sich verneigt.*)
> Von meiner Herrin?
> Ihr gehorsam
> was zu hören
> meldet höfisch
> mir die traute Magd?

BRANGÄNE:

> Mein Herre Tristan,
> Euch zu sehen
> wünscht Isolde,
> meine Frau.

TRISTAN:

> Grämt sie die lange Fahrt,
> die geht zu End';
> eh noch die Sonne sinkt,
> sind wir am Land.
> Was meine Frau mir befehle,
> treulich sei's erfüllt.

BRANGÄNE:

> So mög' Herr Tristan
> zu ihr gehn:
> das ist der Herrin Will'.

TRISTAN:

> Wo dort die grünen Fluren
> dem Blick noch blau sich färben,
> harrt mein König
> meiner Frau:
> zu ihm sie zu geleiten,
> bald nah' ich mich der Lichten;
> keinem gönnt' ich
> diese Gunst.

BRANGÄNE:

> Mein Herre Tristan,
> höre wohl:
> deine Dienste
> will die Frau,
> daß du zur Stell' ihr nahtest
> dort, wo sie deiner harrt.

KURVENAL (*sees Brangaene coming, and plucks Tristan by the robe without rising*):

Beware, Tristan!
Message from Isolde.

TRISTAN (*starting*):

What's that? Isolde?

He quickly masters himself as Brangaene approaches and curtsies.

You're from my lady?
Does she give you
courtly orders
brought this servant
by her faithful maid?

BRANGAENE:

My lord, Sir Tristan,
Dame Isolde
wishes you to
come to her.

TRISTAN:

Her journey must seem long
but soon will end.
Before the sun has set
we'll be ashore.
Let but my lady command me:
straight it shall be done.

BRANGAENE:

Let then Lord Tristan
go to her:
that is the lady's will.

TRISTAN:

There, where the grassy meadows
to sight look blue in color,
there my master
waits my dame:
I soon must see the Bright One
and lead her to my sov'reign;
there's no other
favored so.

BRANGAENE:

My master Tristan,
listen well:
since your service
is required,

TRISTAN: Auf jeder Stelle,
                    wo ich steh',
                    getreulich dien' ich ihr,
                    der Frauen höchster Ehr;
                    ließ' ich das Steuer
                    jetzt zur Stund',
                    wie lenkt' ich sicher den Kiel
                    zu König Markes Land?

BRANGÄNE: Tristan, mein Herre!
                    Was höhnst du mich?
                    Dünkt dich nicht deutlich
                    die tör'ge Magd,
                    hör meiner Herrin Wort!
                    So, hieß sie, sollt' ich sagen:
                    Befehlen ließ'
                    dem Eigenholde
                    Furcht der Herrin
                    sie, Isolde.

KURWENAL *(aufspringend)*:
                    Darf ich die Antwort sagen?

TRISTAN *(ruhig)*: Was wohl erwidertest du?

KURWENAL: Das sage sie
                    der Frau Isold'!
                    Wer Kornwalls Kron'
                    und Englands Erb'
                    an Irlands Maid vermacht,
                    der kann der Magd
                    nicht eigen sein,
                    die selbst dem Ohm er schenkt.
                    Ein Herr der Welt
                    Tristan der Held!
                    Ich ruf's: du sag's, und grollten
                    mir tausend Frau Isolden!
                    *(Da Tristan durch Gebärden ihm zu wehren
                    sucht und Brangäne entrüstet sich zum
                    Weggehen wendet, singt Kurwenal der
                    zögernd sich Entfernenden mit höchster
                    Stärke nach:)*

my mistress asks your presence
there where she waits for you.

TRISTAN:

I give my duty
where I stand,
in service ever true
to her of crowning name.
If I this instant
left the helm,
how could I safely direct
the ship to King Mark's land?

BRANGAENE:

Tristan, my master!
Why mock at me?
If words are cloudy
from foolish maid,
hark to my lady's words.
Thus, said she, should I tell you:
"Just let this lord
so self-sufficient,
fear his mistress,
me, Isolde!"

KURVENAL *(springing up)*:

Dare I supply the answer?

TRISTAN *(calmly)*:

What kind of answer have you?

KURVENAL:

This let her say
to Dame Isolde:
If Cornwall's crown
and England's fee
to Ireland's maid are made,
he cannot be
the chattel of
the prize he brings his lord.
A lord world-famed,
Tristan the great!
I've said: despite complaining
from a thousand Dame Isoldes.

*While Tristan by gestures tries to silence
him, and Brangaene, offended, turns to go
away, Kurvenal, as she slowly moves away,
sings after her at the top of his voice.*

„Herr Morold zog
zu Meere her,
in Kornwall Zins zu haben;
ein Eiland schwimmt
auf ödem Meer,
da liegt er nun begraben!
Sein Haupt doch hängt
im Irenland,
als Zins gezahlt
von Engeland:
Hei! Unser Held Tristan,
wie der Zins zahlen kann!"
*(Kurwenal, von Tristan fortgescholten, ist in
den Schiffsraum hinabgestiegen; Brangäne
in Bestürzung zu Isolde zurückgekehrt,
schließt hinter sich die Vorhänge, während
die ganze Mannschaft außen sich hören
läßt.)*

ALLE MÄNNER: Sein Haupt doch hängt
im Irenland,
als Zins gezahlt
von Engeland:
Hei! Unser Held Tristan,
wie der Zins zahlen kann!

DRITTER AUFTRITT

*Isolde und Brangäne allein, bei vollkommen wieder geschlos-
senen Vorhängen. — Isolde erhebt sich mit verzweiflungsvoller
Wutgebärde. Brangäne stürzt ihr zu Füßen.*

BRANGÄNE: Weh, ach wehe!
Dies zu dulden!

ISOLDE *(dem furchtbarsten Ausbruche nahe, schnell sich
zusammenraffend):*
Doch nun von Tristan!
Genau will ich's vernehmen.

BRANGÄNE: Ach, frage nicht!

ISOLDE: Frei sag's ohne Furcht!

"Lord Morold crossed
the wat'ry wave,
for Cornish tax he harried;
a lonely island
holds his grave,
where he lies now quite buried!
His head now hangs
in Irish land,
the tax returned
by Engeland:
Here's to our lord Tristan,
for the tax, what a man!"

Kurvenal, driven away by Tristan, goes be-
low to the cabin; Brangaene, much disturbed,
returns to Isolde, and closes the curtains be-
hind her while the whole crew is heard
singing without.

ALL THE MEN: "His head now hangs
in Irish land,
the tax returned
by Engeland:
Here's to our lord Tristan,
for the tax, what a man!"

SCENE III

Isolde and Brangaene alone; the curtains are again completely
closed. Isolde rises with a despairing gesture of wrath. Bran-
gaene falls at her feet.

BRANGAENE: Woe! What sorrow
must be suffered!

ISOLDE *(restraining herself from a furious outbreak)*:
What now of Tristan?
I wish to know exactly.

BRANGAENE: Ah, do not ask!

ISOLDE: Speak out without fear.

BRANGÄNE: Mit höf'schen Worten
                   wich er aus.

ISOLDE: Doch als du deutlich mahntest?

BRANGÄNE: Da ich zur Stell'
                   ihn zu dir rief:
                   wo er auch steh',
                   so sagte er,
                   getreulich dien' er ihr,
                   der Frauen höchster Ehr';
                   ließ' er das Steuer
                   jetzt zur Stund',
                   wie lenkt' er sicher den Kiel
                   zu König Markes Land?

ISOLDE *(schmerzlich bitter)*:
                   „Wie lenkt' er sicher den Kiel
                   zu König Markes Land?" *(Grell und heftig.)*
                   Den Zins ihm auszuzahlen,
                   den er aus Irland zog!

BRANGÄNE: Auf deine eignen Worte,
                   als ich ihm die entbot,
                   ließ seinen Treuen Kurwenal —

ISOLDE: Den hab' ich wohl vernommen,
                   kein Wort, was mir entging.
                   Erfuhrest du meine Schmach,
                   nun höre, was sie mir schuf.
                   Wie lachend sie
                   mir Lieder singen,
                   wohl könnt' auch ich erwidern
                   von einem Kahn,
                   der klein und arm
                   an Irlands Küste schwamm,
                   darinnen krank
                   ein siecher Mann
                   elend im Sterben lag.
                   Isolde Kunst
                   ward ihm bekannt;
                   mit Heilsalben
                   und Balsamsaft
                   der Wunde, die ihn plagte,
                   getreulich pflag sie da.

BRANGAENE: His courtly phrases
              told no tale.

ISOLDE: But when you plainly asked him?

BRANGAENE: When I had plainly
              bid him come:
              just where he stands,
              he said to me,
              he truly serves you well,
              this pearl of womanhood;
              if he this instant
              left the helm,
              how could he safely direct
              the boat to King Mark's land?

ISOLDE (*bitterly*):
                   "How could he safely direct
                   the boat to King Mark's land?"
                   To pay the tax again
                   that he brings from Ireland's realm!

BRANGAENE: When I announced your message
              and in your very words,
              then did his servant Kurvenal . . .

ISOLDE: That did I hear quite clearly;
              I did not miss a word.
              My maid has witnessed my shame;
              now listen how it was wrought.
              They sing derisive
              songs against me.
              Yet I could well requite them:
              about a boat
              both small and mean
              that sailed to Ireland's coast;
              and there, within,
              a man lay sick,
              wretched, at point of death.
              Isolde's skill
              became his help.
              Her salves soothed him,
              and healing balms;
              the wounds from which he suffered
              she tended faithfully.

Der „Tantris"
mit sorgender List sich nannte,
als Tristan
Isold' ihn bald erkannte,
da in des Müß'gen Schwerte
eine Scharte sie gewahrte,
darin genau
sich fügt' ein Splitter,
den einst im Haupt
des Iren-Ritter,
zum Hohn ihr heimgesandt,
mit kund'ger Hand sie fand.
Da schrie's mir auf
aus tiefstem Grund!
Mit dem hellen Schwert
ich vor ihm stund,
an ihm, dem Überfrechen,
Herrn Morolds Tod zu rächen.
Von seinem Lager
blickt' er her —
nicht auf das Schwert,
nicht auf die Hand —
er sah mir in die Augen.
Seines Elendes
jammerte mich! —
Das Schwert — ich ließ es fallen!
Die Morold schlug, die Wunde,
sie heilt' ich, daß er gesunde
und heim nach Hause kehre —
mit dem Blick mich nicht mehr beschwere!

BRANGÄNE: O Wunder! Wo hatt' ich die Augen?
                 Der Gast, den einst
                 ich pflegen half?

ISOLDE: Sein Lob hörest du eben:
                 „Hei! Unser Held Tristan" —
                 der war jener traur'ge Mann.
                 Er schwur mit tausend Eiden
                 mir ew'gen Dank und Treue!
                 Nun hör, wie ein Held
                 Eide hält!
                 Den als Tantris

Most slyly
he went by the name of "Tantris,"
but soon Isold'
knew the man as Tristan,
when in his idle weapon
she observed a nick that marred it,
in which a splinter
fit exactly,
that in the head
of Ireland's hero,
sent home to her in scorn,
she'd found with cunning hand.
Then came a cry
from deep within!
Facing him I stood
with that bright sword,
to slay the overbold one,
and venge the death of Morold.
Then from his pallet
Tristan looked,
not on the sword,
nor at my hand,—
his eyes met mine directly;
and his misery
troubled my heart.
The sword—my hand just dropped it.
The wound he had from Morold,
I healed it, that, well in body,
he'd seek his home and leave me,
and with glances no more disturb me.

BRANGAENE: A wonder! Till now was I blinded?
The guest whom once
I helped to tend?

ISOLDE: Just now you heard his praises:
"Hail to the brave Tristan"—
he was that poor, wretched man.
A thousand oaths he swore me
of endless thanks and homage!
Now hear how a knight
holds his oath!
Who as Tantris,

unerkannt ich entlassen,
als Tristan
kehrt' er kühn zurück;
auf stolzem Schiff,
von hohem Bord,
Irlands Erbin
begehrt' er zur Eh'
für Kornwalls müden König,
für Marke, seinen Ohm.
Da Morold lebte,
wer hätt' es gewagt
uns je solche Schmach zu bieten?
Für der zinspflicht'gen
Kornen Fürsten
um Irlands Krone zu werben!
Ach, wehe mir!
Ich ja war's,
die heimlich selbst
die Schmach sich schuf!
Das rächende Schwert,
statt es zu schwingen,
machtlos ließ ich's fallen!
Nun dien' ich dem Vasallen!

BRANGÄNE: Da Friede, Sühn' und Freundschaft
von allen ward beschworen,
wir freuten uns all' des Tags;
wie ahnte mir da,
daß dir es Kummer schüf'?

ISOLDE: O blinde Augen!
Blöde Herzen!
Zahmer Mut,
verzagtes Schweigen!
Wie anders prahlte
Tristan aus,
was ich verschlossen hielt!
Die schweigend ihm
das Leben gab,
vor Feindes Rache
ihn schweigend barg;
was stumm ihr Schutz
zum Heil ihm schuf —

unbeknown, gets his freedom,
as Tristan
boldly came again.
His ship was proud,
with lofty deck,
and he sought
Ireland's heiress as bride
for Cornwall's weary monarch,—
his uncle, who is Mark.
With Morold living,
whoever would dare
to make such affront upon us?
For that taxpaying
Cornish king
thinks to win Ireland's crown as suitor.
Ah, woe is me!
I it was
myself who wrought
my secret shame!
The sword of revenge
would not be wielded;
weakly I just dropped it.
So now I serve my vassal.

BRANGAENE: When concord, peace, and friendship
were sworn by all the parties,
that day did we all rejoice;
how could I suspect
the pain that it would cause?

ISOLDE: O eyes that see not!
Hearts so timid!
Spirit tamed,
despairing silence!
Quite otherwise he
prattled forth
what I had never breathed.
The one whose silence
spared his life,
who kept him safely
from vengeful foes;
The silent shelter
owed to her—

mit ihr gab er es preis!
Wie siegprangend
heil und hehr,
laut und hell
wies er auf mich:
,,Das wär' ein Schatz,
mein Herr und Ohm;
wie dünkt Euch die zur Eh'?
Die schmucke Irin
hol' ich her;
mit Steg' und Wegen
wohlbekannt,
ein Wink, ich flieg'
nach Irenland:
Isolde, die ist Euer! —
Mir lacht das Abenteuer!"
Fluch dir, Verruchter!
Fluch deinem Haupt!
Rache! Tod!
Tod uns beiden!

BRANGÄNE (*mit ungestümer Zärtlichkeit auf Isolde stürzend*):
O Süße! Traute!
Teure! Holde!
Goldne Herrin!
Lieb' Isolde!
(*Sie zieht Isolde allmählich nach dem Ruhebett.*)
Hör mich! Komme!
Setz dich her!
Welcher Wahn!
Welch eitles Zürnen!
Wie magst du dich betören,
nicht hell zu sehn noch hören?
Was je Herr Tristan
dir verdankte,
sag, konnt' er's höher lohnen
als mit der herrlichsten der Kronen?
So dient' er treu
dem edlen Ohm;
dir gab er der Welt
begehrlichsten Lohn:

with her—he dared betray!
How, vic'try-flushed,
hale, sublime,
strong, he
indicated me:
"A treasure, sure,
my lord and uncle;
how does she suit as bride?
I'll fetch the pretty
Irish lass;
just nod, I'll fly
to Irish land
by roads and ways well
known to me.
Isolde shall be yours, sire!
I joy in this adventure!"
Curse you, you dastard!
Cursed be your head!
Vengeance! Death!
Let us both die!

BRANGAENE (*throwing herself upon Isolde with impetuous tenderness*):

O sweet one! Loved one!
Darling! Precious!
Golden lady!
Dear Isolde!
(*She gradually draws Isolde toward the couch.*)
Hear me! Come now!
Sit down here!
What a dream!
What idle raving!
Why be so self-deceiving
as not to see or listen?
No matter what Sir Tristan
owes you,
how better could he pay you
than with this noblest crown of glory?
Thus does he serve
his uncle well;
he gives you the world's
most coveted prize:

dem eignen Erbe,
echt und edel,
entsagt' er zu deinen Füßen,
als Königin dich zu grüßen!
(Isolde wendet sich ab.)
Und warb er Marke
dir zum Gemahl,
wie wolltest du die Wahl doch schelten,
muß er nicht wert dir gelten?
Von edler Art
und mildem Mut,
wer gliche dem Mann
an Macht und Glanz?
Dem ein hehrster Held
so treulich dient,
wer möchte sein Glück nicht teilen,
als Gattin bei ihm weilen?

ISOLDE *(starr vor sich hinblickend)*:
Ungeminnt
den hehrsten Mann
stets mir nah zu sehen!
Wie könnt' ich die Qual bestehen?

BRANGÄNE:
Was wähnst du, Arge?
Ungeminnt? —
*(Sie nähert sich schmeichelnd und kosend
Isolden.)*
Wo lebte der Mann,
der dich nicht liebte?
Der Isolden säh'
und in Isolden
selig nicht ganz verging'?
Doch, der dir erkoren,
wär' er so kalt,
zög ihn von dir
ein Zauber ab:
den bösen wüßt' ich
bald zu binden.
Ihn bannte der Minne Macht.
*(Mit geheimnisvoller Zutraulichkeit ganz zu
Isolde.)*
Kennst du der Mutter
Künste nicht?

all he's heir to,
truly noble,
renouncing, to place his treasure
at feet of the queen he honors.

Isolde turns away.

And if through Tristan
you wed King Mark,
why should you find fault with the choice?
Is he one not worth the prizing?
Of noble line
and gentle strength,
who equals this man
in might and fame?
Whom so great a knight
so truly serves,
who would not then share his fortune,
and dwell with such a husband?

ISOLDE *(staring vacantly)*:
Unbeloved,
yet ever near
this unrivaled hero!
How could I endure the torment?

BRANGAENE:
What's that, perverse one?
Unbeloved?
(She approaches Isolde coaxingly and caress-ingly.)
Where lives there a man
that would not love you?
Who that saw Isolde
would not, seeing,
dissolve in love for her?
Yet, him that is chosen,
even if cold,
drawn from your side
by magic arts,
him, though unkind,
I soon would shackle
and thrall with a mighty love.
(Coming close to Isolde with mysterious familiarity.)
Do you not know
your mother's arts?

Wähnst du, die alles
klug erwägt,
ohne Rat in fremdes Land
hätt' sie mit dir mich entsandt?

ISOLDE *(düster)*: Der Mutter Rat
gemahnt mich recht:
willkommen preis' ich
ihre Kunst: —
Rache für den Verrat —
Ruh' in der Not dem Herzen!
Den Schrein dort bring mir her!

BRANGÄNE: Er birgt, was Heil dir frommt.
*(Sie holt eine kleine goldne Truhe herbei,
öffnet sie und deutet auf ihren Inhalt.)*
So reihte sie die Mutter,
die mächt'gen Zaubertränke.
Für Weh und Wunden
Balsam hier;
für böse Gifte
Gegengift. *(Sie zieht ein Fläschchen hervor.)*
Den hehrsten Trank,
ich halt' ihn hier.

ISOLDE: Du irrst, ich kenn' ihn besser;
ein starkes Zeichen,
schnitt ich ihm ein.
(Sie ergreift ein Fläschchen und zeigt es.)
Der Trank ist's, der mir taugt!

BRANGÄNE *(weicht entsetzt zurück)*:
Der Todestrank!
*(Isolde hat sich vom Ruhebett erhoben und
vernimmt mit wachsendem Schrecken den
Ruf des Schiffsvolks.)*

SCHIFFSVOLK *(von außen)*:
Ho! He! Ha! He!
Am Untermast
die Segel ein!
Ho! He! Ha! He!

ISOLDE: Das deutet schnelle Fahrt.
Weh mir! Nahe das Land!
*(Durch die Vorhänge tritt mit Ungestüm
Kurwenal herein.)*

Think you that she,
who ponders all
would have sent me void of counsel
to this strange land with you?

ISOLDE *(darkly)*: My mother's arts
I well recall;
most gladly I commend
her art.
Vengeance for who betrays,
rest for the troubled bosom!
That casket—bring it here!

BRANGAENE: It hides what does you good.
*(She fetches a small gold box, opens it, and
indicates its contents.)*
Your mother ranged them this way,
these mighty, magic potions.
For woe and wounds
the balsam here;
for deadly poison,
antidote.
(She takes out a small vial.)
The sweetest drink
I hold right here.

ISOLDE: You err, I know one better;
I marked a heavy
sign on the one.
(She seizes a vial and shows it.)
The drink here serves my turn.
*(She has risen from the couch and listens
with rising dread to the cries of the seamen.)*

BRANGAENE *(recoils in horror)*:
The drink of death!

SEAMEN *(without)*: Ho! Hey! Ha! Hey!
Stand by the mast!
Haul in the sail!
Ho! Hey! Ha! Hey!

ISOLDE: How swift our trip has been!
Woe's me! Here is the land!

*Kurvenal boisterously enters through the
curtains.*

VIERTER AUFTRITT

Die Vorigen und Kurwenal.

KURWENAL: Auf! Auf! Ihr Frauen!
Frisch und froh!
Rasch gerüstet!
Fertig nun, hurtig und flink!
(Gemessener.)
Und Frau Isolden
sollt' ich sagen
von Held Tristan,
meinem Herrn:
Vom Mast der Freude Flagge,
sie wehe lustig ins Land;
in Markes Königschlosse
mach' sie ihr Nahn bekannt.
Drum Frau Isolde
bät' er eilen,
fürs Land sich zu bereiten,
daß er sie könnt' geleiten.

ISOLDE *(nachdem sie zuerst bet der Meldung in Schauer zusammengefahren, gefaßt und mit Würde)*:
Herrn Tristan bringe
meinen Gruß
und meld ihm, was ich sage.
Sollt' ich zur Seit' ihm gehen,
vor König Marke zu stehen,
nicht möcht' es nach Zucht
und Fug geschehn,
empfing ich Sühne
nicht zuvor
für ungesühnte Schuld:
Drum such er meine Huld.
(Kurwenal macht eine trotzige Gebärde.)

ISOLDE *(fährt mit Steigerung fort)*:
Du merke wohl
und meld es gut!
Nicht woll' ich mich bereiten,
ans Land ihn zu begleiten;
nicht werd' ich zur Seit' ihm gehen,
vor König Marke zu stehen;
begehrte Vergessen
und Vergeben
nach Zucht und Fug

SCENE IV

KURVENAL:

Up, up, you women!
Bright and spry!
Quickly does it!
Ready and prompt, nimble and brisk!
(Formally.)
For Dame Isolde
comes a message
my lord Tristan
would declare:
upon the mast the pennant
is gaily waving to shore;
within Mark's royal castle
your nearness now is known.
Wherefore he begs
the lady hurry,
get ready for the landing,
that then he may escort her.

ISOLDE *(who was at first startled at the summons, now composedly and with dignity)*:

Sir Tristan has my
greeting now:
inform him what I tell you.
If I'm to walk beside him
to stand before Mark, his monarch,
it may never be
as custom wills,
unless he finds
atonement first
for uncondoned offense:
So let him seek my grace.

Kurvenal makes a gesture of defiance.

Now mark me well,
report it right!
I will not now make ready
to let him hence escort me;
nor shall I parade beside him,
nor stand before Mark his monarch,
till he seek forgiveness
and forgetting
in fitting and

er nicht zuvor
für ungebüßte Schuld:
die böt' ihm meine Huld!

KURWENAL: Sicher wißt,
das sag' ich ihm;
nun harrt, wie er mich hört!
(Er geht schnell zurück. Isolde eilt auf Bran-
gäne zu und umarmt sie heftig.)

ISOLDE: Nun leb wohl, Brangäne!
Grüß mir die Welt,
grüße mir Vater und Mutter!

BRANGÄNE: Was ist? Was sinnst du?
Wolltest du fliehn?
Wohin soll ich dir folgen?

ISOLDE *(faßt sich schnell)*:
Hörtest du nicht?
Hier bleib' ich,
Tristan will ich erwarten.
Getreu befolg,
was ich befehl',
den Sühnetrank
rüste schnell;
du weißt, den ich dir wies?
(Sie entnimmt dem Schrein das Fläschchen.)

BRANGÄNE: Und welchen Trank?

ISOLDE: Diesen Trank!
In die goldne Schale
gieß ihn aus;
gefüllt faßt sie ihn ganz.

BRANGÄNE *(voll Grausen das Fläschchen empfangend)*:
Trau' ich dem Sinn?

ISOLDE: Sei du mir treu!

BRANGÄNE: Den Trank — für wen?

ISOLDE: Wer mich betrog —

BRANGÄNE: Tristan?

ISOLDE: — trinke mir Sühne!

               becoming way
               for unatoned offense:
               then let him hope for grace.

KURVENAL: Rest assured,
               he shall be told;
               Now wait, see how he hears.

               He retires quickly. Isolde hurries to Bran-
               gaene and embraces her warmly.

ISOLDE: Now farewell, Brangaene!
               Greet all for me.
               Greet both my father and mother.

BRANGAENE: What's this? What thoughts, these?
               Would you plan flight?
               To what place shall I follow?

ISOLDE *(quickly collecting herself)*:
               Did you not hear?
               I'm staying.
               Here will I wait for Tristan.
               Just truly
               follow my command:
               prepare the peace
               drink straightway.
               I once showed it to you.
               (She takes the vial from the casket.)

BRANGAENE: Which drink is that?

ISOLDE: Here it is!
               Pour it out into
               the golden cup;
               it just holds it when filled.

BRANGAENE *(taking the vial in terror)*:
               Can this be true?

ISOLDE: Mind you be true!

BRANGAENE: The drink—for whom?

ISOLDE: Him that betrayed.

BRANGAENE: Tristan?

ISOLDE: Let him atone it.

BRANGÄNE *(zu Isoldes Füßen stürzend)*:
Entsetzen! Schone mich Arme!

ISOLDE *(sehr heftig)*:
Schone du mich,
untreue Magd!
Kennst du der Mutter
Künste nicht?
Wähnst du, die alles
klug erwägt,
ohne Rat in fremdes Land
hätt' sie mit dir mich entsandt?
Für Weh und Wunden
gab sie Balsam,
für böse Gifte
Gegen-Gift.
Für tiefstes Weh,
für höchstes Leid
gab sie den Todestrank.
Der Tod nun sag ihr Dank!

BRANGÄNE *(kaum ihrer mächtig)*:
O tiefstes Weh!

ISOLDE:
Gehorchst du mir nun?

BRANGÄNE:
O höchstes Leid!

ISOLDE:
Bist du mir treu?

BRANGÄNE:
Der Trank?

KURWENAL *(eintretend)*:
Herr Tristan!
(Brangäne erhebt sich erschrocken und ver-
wirrt. Isolde sucht mit furchtbarer Anstren-
gung sich zu fassen.)

ISOLDE *(zu Kurwenal)*:
Herr Tristan trete nah!

BRANGAENE *(throwing herself at Isolde's feet):*
> O horror! Spare me, most wretched!

ISOLDE *(very vehemently):*
> Spare me instead,
> disloyal girl!
> Do you not know my
> mother's arts?
> Think you that she, who
> ponders all,
> would have sent me void of counsel
> to this strange land with you?
> For woes and wounds she
> gave a balsam,
> for deadly poisons
> antidote.
> For deepest woe,
> for greatest pain
> death's drink was what she gave.
> Let Death now give her thanks.

BRANGAENE *(almost beside herself):*
> O deepest woe!

ISOLDE: Now will you obey?

BRANGAENE: O greatest pain!

ISOLDE: Will you be true?

BRANGAENE: The drink?

KURVENAL *(entering):*
> Lord Tristan!

> *Brangaene rises, terrified and confused.*
> *Isolde strives with a mighty effort to com-*
> *pose herself.*

ISOLDE *(to Kurvenal):*
> Lord Tristan may approach.

FÜNFTER AUFTRITT

Tristan. Isolde. Brangäne. Später Kurwenal, Schiffsvolk, Ritter
und Knappen.

(Kurwenal geht wieder zurück. Brangäne, kaum ihrer mächtig,
wendet sich in den Hintergrund. Isolde, ihr ganzes Gefühl
zur Entscheidung zusammenfassend, schreitet langsam, mit
großer Haltung, dem Ruhebett zu, auf dessen Kopfende sich
stützend sie den Blick fest dem Eingange zuwendet. — Tristan
tritt ein und bleibt ehrerbietig am Eingange stehen. — Isolde
ist mit furchtbarer Aufregung in seinen Anblick versunken. —
Langes Schweigen.)

TRISTAN: Begehrt, Herrin,
was Ihr wünscht.

ISOLDE: Wüßtest du nicht,
was ich begehre,
da doch die Furcht,
mir's zu erfüllen,
fern meinem Blick dich hielt?

TRISTAN: Ehrfurcht
hielt mich in Acht.

ISOLDE: Der Ehre wenig
botest du mir;
mit offnem Hohn
verwehrtest du
Gehorsam meinem Gebot.

TRISTAN: Gehorsam einzig
hielt mich in Bann.

ISOLDE: So dankt' ich Geringes
deinem Herrn,
riet dir sein Dienst
Unsitte
gegen sein eigen Gemahl?

TRISTAN: Sitte lehrt,
wo ich gelebt:
zur Brautfahrt
der Brautwerber
meide fern die Braut.

Scene V

*Kurvenal retires again. Brangaene, almost beside herself, turns
toward the back. Isolde, summoning all her powers to meet
the crisis, walks slowly and with effort to the couch, leaning
for support on its head. Her eyes are fixed on the entrance.*

*Tristan enters and pauses respectfully at the entrance. Isolde,
a prey to violent agitation, gazes on him intently.*

TRISTAN: Command, Lady,
what you wish.

ISOLDE: Do you not know
just what my wish is,
when fear you had
to undertake it
has kept you from my sight?

TRISTAN: Rev'rence
held me in awe.

ISOLDE: Scant rev'rence truly
have you shown me;
with open scorn
you have refused
obedience to my command.

TRISTAN: Obedience rather
kept me away.

ISOLDE: Small cause would I have to
thank your lord,
if serving him
makes you
discourteous toward his bride.

TRISTAN: Custom asks—
where I have lived:
ere marriage
the bride escort
keep afar from her.

ISOLDE: Aus welcher Sorg'?

TRISTAN: Fragt die Sitte!

ISOLDE: Da du so sittsam,
            mein Herr Tristan,
            auch einer Sitte
            sei nun gemahnt:
            den Feind dir zu sühnen,
            soll er als Freund dich rühmen.

TRISTAN: Und welchen Feind?

ISOLDE: Frag deine Furcht!
            Blutschuld
            schwebt zwischen uns.

TRISTAN: Die ward gesühnt.

ISOLDE: Nicht zwischen uns!

TRISTAN: Im offnen Feld
            vor allem Volk
            ward Urfehde geschworen.

ISOLDE: Nicht da war's,
            wo ich Tantris barg,
            wo Tristan mir verfiel.
            Da stand er herrlich,
            hehr und heil;
            doch was er schwur,
            das schwur ich nicht:
            zu schweigen hatt' ich gelernt.
            Da in stiller Kammer
            krank er lag,
            mit dem Schwerte stumm
            ich vor ihm stund:
            schwieg da mein Mund,
            bannt' ich meine Hand —
            doch was einst mit Hand
            und Mund ich gelobt,
            das schwur ich schweigend zu halten.
            Nun will ich des Eides walten.

TRISTAN: Was schwurt Ihr, Frau?

ISOLDE: Rache für Morold!

ISOLDE:	And on what grounds?
TRISTAN:	Ask of custom!
ISOLDE:	Since you're for custom, my lord Tristan, one other custom you should recall: for foe to be friendly, let him count you as friendly.
TRISTAN:	And who's the foe?
ISOLDE:	Ask of your fear. Bloodguilt stands in the way.
TRISTAN:	That was made good.
ISOLDE:	Not between us.
TRISTAN:	In open field before all folk a peace compact was sworn to.
ISOLDE:	But that was not where Tantris hid nor Tristan fell to me. He stood there lordly, strong and hale; yet what he swore I did not swear: I'd learned that silence was best. As he lay there in my chamber sick, mute I stood before him with my sword: Silent my lips, motionless my hand— yet what once I'd pledged with hand and by mouth, I swore to harbor in silence. Now will I perform that promise.
TRISTAN:	What did you swear?
ISOLDE:	Vengeance for Morold!

TRISTAN: Müht Euch die?

ISOLDE: Wagst du zu höhnen?
                Angelobt war er mir,
                der hehre Irenheld;
                seine Waffen hatt' ich geweiht;
                für mich zog er zum Streit.
                Da er gefallen,
                fiel meine Ehr':
                in des Herzens Schwere
                schwur ich den Eid,
                würd' ein Mann den Mord nicht sühnen,
                wollt' ich Magd mich des erkühnen.
                Siech und matt
                in meiner Macht,
                warum ich dich da nicht schlug?
                Das sag dir selbst mit leichtem Fug.
                Ich pflag des Wunden,
                daß den Heilgesunden
                rächend schlüge der Mann,
                der Isolden ihm abgewann.
                Dein Los nun selber
                magst du dir sagen!
                Da die Männer sich all ihm vertragen,
                wer muß nun Tristan schlagen?

TRISTAN *(bleich und düster)*:
                War Morold dir so wert,
                nun wieder nimm das Schwert
                und führ es sicher und fest,
                daß du nicht dir's entfallen läßt!
                (Er reicht ihr sein Schwert dar.)

ISOLDE: Wie sorgt' ich schlecht
                um deinen Herren;
                was würde König Marke sagen,
                erschlüg' ich ihm
                den besten Knecht,
                der Kron' und Land ihm gewann,
                den allertreusten Mann?
                Dünkt dich so wenig,
                was er dir dankt,
                bringst du die Irin
                ihm als Braut,

TRISTAN: Are you concerned?

ISOLDE: Dare you to mock me?
He was fianced to me,
that gallant Irish lord;
I had consecrated his arms;
for me he went to war.
Then, with his downfall
my honor fell;
when my heart was heavy
this vow I swore:
if no man avenged his murder,
I, a maid, would dare to do so.
Sick and weak
and in my power,
why I did not slay you there,
explain yourself with easy words:
his wound I tended
so the one so healed might
pay his life to the man
who had won Isolde for bride.
Yourself may tell the
fate you're allotted.
As the men are all at peace with Tristan,
who is there left to smite him?

TRISTAN *(pale and gloomy)*:
If Morold meant so much,
then take the sword again,
and drive it surely and straight,
that it may not escape your grasp.
(He offers her his sword.)

ISOLDE: How bad a turn
to do your master!
How do you think King Mark would take it,
if I struck down
his best of knights,
who won him both crown and land,
his truest man of all?
Think you his cause to
thank you so small,
when you have brought his
Irish bride,

daß er nicht schölte,
schlüg' ich den Werber,
der Urfehde-Pfand
so treu ihm liefert zur Hand?
Wahre dein Schwert!
Da einst ich's schwang,
als mir die Rache
im Busen rang:
als dein messender Blick
mein Bild sich stahl,
ob ich Herrn Marke
taug' als Gemahl:
Das Schwert — da ließ ich's sinken.
Nun laß uns Sühne trinken!
*(Sie winkt Brangäne. Diese schaudert zusam-
men, schwankt und zögert in ihrer Bewe-
gung. Isolde treibt sie mit gesteigerter
Gebärde an. Brangäne läßt sich zur Bereit-
ung des Trankes an.)*

SCHIFFSVOLK *(von außen)*:
Ho! He! Ha! He!
Am Obermast
die Segel ein!
Ho! He! Ha! He!

TRISTAN *(aus düsterem Brüten auffahrend)*:
Wo sind wir?

ISOLDE: Hart am Ziel!
Tristan, gewinn' ich Sühne?
Was hast du mir zu sagen?

TRISTAN *(finster)*:
Des Schweigens Herrin
heißt mich schweigen:
fass' ich, was sie verschweig,
verschweig' ich, was sie nicht faßt.

ISOLDE: Dein Schweigen fass' ich,
weichst du mir aus.
Weigerst du die Sühne mir?

SCHIFFSVOLK *(von außen)*:
Ho! He! Ha! He!
*(Auf Isoldes ungeduldigen Wink reicht Bran-
gäne ihr die gefüllte Trinkschale.)*

he would not chide
if I slew the wooer
who faithfully brings
this peace hostage to your hand?
Put up your sword!
I grasped it once,
when thoughts of vengeance
had rent my heart,
when your measuring glance
could truly tell
whether I'd serve as
bride for King Mark:
I let the sword fall from me.
Now let us drink our friendship.

She signs to Brangaene, who cowers and trembles as she moves. Isolde urges her with more impatient gestures. Brangaene sets about preparing the drink.

VOICES OF THE SAILORS *(without)*:
Ho! Hey! Ha! Hey!
Stand by the mast!
Haul down the sail!
Ho! Hey! Ha! Hey!

TRISTAN *(starting from his moody silence)*:
Where are we?

ISOLDE:
Near our goal.
Tristan, what satisfaction?
What do you have to tell me?

TRISTAN *(darkly)*:
The queen of silence
asks for silence:
grasping what she conceals,
I hide, though, what she can't grasp.

ISOLDE:
I grasp your silence
though you elude me.
Do you then refuse to pledge?

SAILORS *(without)*:
Ho! Hey! Ha! Hey!

On an impatient sign from Isolde, Brangaene hands her the full goblet.

ISOLDE *(mit dem Becher zu Tristan tretend, der ihr starr in die Augen blickt)*:

> Du hörst den Ruf?
> Wir sind am Ziel.
> In kurzer Frist
> stehn wir *(mit leisem Hohne)*
> vor König Marke.
> Geleitest du mich,
> dünkt dich's nicht lieb,
> darfst du so ihm sagen:
> „Mein Herr und Ohm,
> sieh die dir an:
> ein sanftres Weib
> gewännst du nie.
> Ihren Angelobten
> erschlug ich ihr einst,
> sein Haupt sandt' ich ihr heim;
> die Wunde, die
> seine Wehr mir schuf,
> die hat sie hold geheilt.
> Mein Leben lag
> in ihrer Macht:
> das schenkte mir
> die holde Magd,
> und ihres Landes
> Schand' und Schmach
> die gab sie mit darein,
> dein Ehgemahl zu sein.
> So guter Gaben
> holden Dank
> schuf mir ein süßer
> Sühnetrank;
> den bot mir ihre Huld,
> zu sühnen alle Schuld."

SCHIFFSVOLK *(außen)*:

> Auf das Tau!
> Anker los!

TRISTAN *(wild auffahrend)*:

> Los den Anker!
> Das Steuer dem Strom!
> Den Winden Segel und Mast! —
> *(Er entreißt ihr die Trinkschale.)*

ISOLDE (*advancing with the cup to Tristan, who gazes fixedly
    in her eyes*):

> You hear the cries?
> We have arrived:
> King Mark will soon
> see us *(with light scorn)*
> standing before him.
> And when I am there,
> were it not well,
> could you thus inform him:
> "My lord and king,
> look at her well:
> a gentler wife
> was never won.
> Her affianced lover
> I slew on a time;
> I sent her home his head:
> The wound that he
> gave me with his sword,
> she graciously made whole;
> my life was fully
> in her power:
> the gentle maid
> allowed that life,
> allowed as well with
> equal ease
> her land's disgrace and shame,
> to be your bride and queen;
> in gracious thanks for
> goodly gifts
> mixed me a pleasant
> drink of peace;
> this way she showed her grace,
> and wiped away my guilt."

SAILORS (*without*):

> Cable up!
> Anchor free!

TRISTAN (*starting wildly*):

> Drop the anchor!
> The helm to the stream!
> The sail and mast to the wind!
> *(He snatches the cup from her.)*

Wohl kenn' ich Irlands
Königin
und ihrer Künste
Wunderkraft.
Den Balsam nützt' ich,
den sie bot:
den Becher nehm' ich nun,
daß ganz ich heut genese.
Und achte auch
des Sühne-Eids,
den ich zum Dank dir sage!
Tristans Ehre —
höchste Treu'!
Tristans Elend —
kühnster Trotz!
Trug des Herzens!
Traum der Ahnung!
Ew'ger Trauer
einz'ger Trost:
Vergessens güt'ger Trank —
dich trink' ich sonder Wank!
(Er setzt an und trinkt.)

ISOLDE: Betrug auch hier?
Mein die Hälfte!
(Sie entwindet ihm den Becher.)
Verräter! Ich trink' sie dir!
*(Sie trinkt. Dann wirft sie die Schale fort.
Beide, von Schauer erfaßt, blicken sich mit
höchster Aufregung, doch mit starrer Haltung, unverwandt in die Augen, in deren
Ausdruck der Todestrotz bald der Liebesglut
weicht. Zittern ergreift sie. Sie fassen sich
krampfhaft an das Herz und führen die
Hand wieder an die Stirn. Dann suchen sie
sich wieder mit dem Blick, senken ihn
verwirrt und heften ihn wieder mit steigen-
der Sehnsucht aufeinander.)*

ISOLDE *(mit bebender Stimme)*:
Tristan!

TRISTAN *(überströmend)*:
Isolde!

Well known to me is
Ireland's queen,
and all her cunning,
wondrous arts.
She proffered balsam,
which I used:
I'll take this beaker now
completely to recover.
Attend then to
my pledge of peace,
that thankfully I offer.
Tristan's honor—
highest faith!
Tristan's anguish—
boldest spite!
Heart's delusion!
Dream of boding!
Endless sorrow's
only rest:
Oblivion's goodly drink!
I pledge you, shrinking not!
(He puts the cup to his lips and drinks.)

ISOLDE: Betrayed here too?
Half is mine now!
(She wrests the cup from him.)
Betrayer! I drink to you!

*She drinks, then throws away the cup. Both,
seized with shuddering, gaze with deepest
emotion, but without changing their position,
while their death-defiant expression changes
to the glow of passion. Trembling seizes
them; they convulsively clutch their hearts
and pass their hands over their brows. Their
glances again seek to meet, sink in confusion,
and once more turn with growing longing
upon each other.*

(With trembling voice.)
Tristan!

TRISTAN *(with an outburst)*:
Isolde!

ISOLDE *(an seine Brust sinkend)*:
                Treuloser Holder!

TRISTAN *(mit Glut sie umfassend)*:
                Seligste Frau!
                (Sie verbleiben in stummer Umarmung. Aus
                der Ferne vernimmt man Trompeten.)

RUF DER MÄNNER *(von außen auf dem Schiffe)*:
                Heil! König Marke Heil!

BRANGÄNE *(die, mit abgewandtem Gesicht, voll Verwirrung
und Schauder sich über den Bord gelehnt hatte, wendet sich
jetzt dem Anblick des in Liebesumarmung versunkenen
Paares zu und stürzt händeringend voll Verzweiflung in den
Vordergrund)*:
                Wehe! Weh!
                Unabwendbar
                ew'ge Not
                für kurzen Tod!
                Tör'ger Treue
                trugvolles Werk
                blüht nun jammernd empor!
                (Tristan und Isolde fahren aus der Umarm-
                ung auf.)

TRISTAN *(verwirrt)*:
                Was träumte mir
                von Tristans Ehre?

ISOLDE:
                Was träumte mir
                von Isoldes Schmach?

TRISTAN:
                Du mir verloren?

ISOLDE:
                 Du mich verstoßen?

TRISTAN:
                Trügenden Zaubers
                tückische List!

ISOLDE:
                Törigen Zürnens
                eitles Dräun!

TRISTAN:
                Isolde!

ISOLDE:
                Tristan!

ISOLDE (*sinking upon his breast*):
>Faithless beloved!

TRISTAN (*he embraces her passionately*):
>Woman most blest!

>*They remain in silent embrace.*
>*Trumpets are heard in the distance.*

ALL THE MEN (*without*):
>Hail to King Mark, all hail!

>*Brangaene, who with averted face was lean-*
>*ing bewildered and trembling over the side*
>*of the ship, now turns and sees the lovers*
>*clasped in each other's arms, and rushes*
>*forward, wringing her hands in despair.*

BRANGAENE:
>Woe is me!
>Here is fatal,
>endless woe
>for speedy death!
>Foolish, faithful
>fraudulent work
>blooms in wails to the skies!

>*Both start from their embrace.*

TRISTAN (*confused*):
>What have I dreamt
>of Tristan's honor?

ISOLDE:
>What have I dreamt
>of Isolde's shame?

TRISTAN:
>You—did I lose you?

ISOLDE:
>You—to repulse me?

TRISTAN:
>Fraudulent magic's
>devilish guile!

ISOLDE:
>Idiot anger's
>empty threats!

TRISTAN:
>Isolde!

ISOLDE:
>Tristan!

TRISTAN: Süßeste Maid!

ISOLDE: Trautester Mann!

BEIDE: Wie sich die Herzen
                    wogend erheben!
                    Wie alle Sinne
                    wonnig erbeben!
                    Sehnender Minne
                    schwellendes Blühen,
                    schmachtender Liebe
                    seliges Glühen!
                    Jach in der Brust
                    jauchzende Lust!
                    Isolde! Tristan!
                    Welten-entronnen,
                    du mir gewonnen!
                    Du mir einzig bewußt,
                    höchste Liebeslust!
                    (Die Vorhänge werden weit auseinandergeris-
                    sen; das ganze Schiff ist mit Rittern und
                    Schiffsvolk bedeckt, die jubelnd über Bord
                    winken, dem Ufer zu, das man, mit einer
                    hohen Felsenburg gekrönt, nahe erblickt. —
                    Tristan und Isolde bleiben, in ihrem gegen-
                    seitigen Anblick verloren, ohne Wahrneh-
                    mung des um sie Vorgehenden.)

BRANGÄNE *(zu den Frauen, die auf ihren Wink aus dem*
    Schiffsraum heraufsteigen):
                    Schnell, den Mantel,
                    den Königsschmuck!
                    (Zwischen Tristan und Isolde stürzend.)
                    Unsel'ge! Auf!
                    Hört, wo wir sind!
                    (Sie legt Isolden, die es nicht gewahrt, den
                    Königsmantel an.)

ALLE MÄNNER: Heil! Heil! Heil!
                    König Marke Heil!
                    Heil dem König!

KURWENAL *(lebhaft herantretend):*
                    Heil Tristan!
                    Glücklicher Held!

TRISTAN: Sweetest of maids!

ISOLDE: Truest of men!

BOTH: Ah, how our hearts are
surging and heaving;
How every sense is
joyfully throbbing!
Passionate longing,
growing and blooming;
languishing love so
blessedly glowing,
bringing my breast
jubilant joy!
Isolde! Tristan!
World, I escape you;
now I have won you,
Tristan! Isolde!
You alone do I know!
Greatest joy of love!

*The curtains are drawn wide apart; the whole
ship is covered with knights and sailors who,
with shouts of joy, make signs to the shore,
which is now seen close at hand, crowned
with a castle. Tristan and Isolde remain ab-
sorbed in mutual contemplation, perceiving
nothing that is passing.*

BRANGAENE (*to the women who, at a signal from her, are com-
ing up from the cabin*):
Quick, the mantle,
the royal robe!
(*Rushing between Tristan and Isolde.*)
Come, unblest pair!
Hear where we are!
(*She puts the royal mantle on Isolde without
her noticing it.*)

ALL THE MEN: Hail! Hail! Hail!
Hail to King Mark, all hail!

KURVENAL (*entering briskly*):
Hail, Tristan!
Hero most blest!

Mit reichem Hofgesinde
dort auf Nachen
naht Herr Marke.
Hei! Wie die Fahrt ihn freut,
daß er die Braut sich freit!

TRISTAN *(in Verwirrung aufblickend)*:
Wer naht?

KURWENAL: Der König!

TRISTAN: Welcher König?
(Kurwenal deutet über Bord.)

ALLE MÄNNER *(die Hüte schwenkend)*:
Heil! König Marke Heil!
(Tristan starrt wie sinnlos nach dem Lande.)

ISOLDE *(in Verwirrung)*:
Was ist, Brangäne?
Welcher Ruf?

BRANGÄNE: Isolde! Herrin!
Fassung nur heut!

ISOLDE: Wo bin ich? Leb' ich?
Ha! Welcher Trank?

BRANGÄNE *(verzweiflungsvoll)*:
Der Liebestrank.

ISOLDE *(starrt entsetzt auf Tristan)*:
Tristan!

TRISTAN: Isolde!

ISOLDE: Muß ich leben?
(Sie stürzt ohnmächtig an seine Brust.)

BRANGÄNE *(zu den Frauen)*:
Helft der Herrin!

TRISTAN: O Wonne voller Tücke!
O truggeweihtes Glücke!

He comes with rich retainers;
there aboard a barge
King Mark comes.
Hey, how well pleased he is,
coming to get his bride!

TRISTAN (*looking up confused*):
Who comes?

KURVENAL: The sov'reign!

TRISTAN: Yes? What sov'reign?

Kurvenal points over the side.

ALL THE MEN (*waving their hats*):
Hail! Hail to Mark the King!

Tristan gazes blankly toward the shore.

ISOLDE (*in confusion*):
What's this, Brangaene?
Why these cries?

BRANGAENE: Isolde! Mistress!
For once be calm!

ISOLDE: Where am I? Living?
What was that drink?

BRANGAENE (*with despair*):
The drink of love!

Isolde stares in terror at Tristan.

ISOLDE: Tristan!

TRISTAN: Isolde!

ISOLDE: Must I live then?
(*She sinks fainting on his breast.*)

BRANGAENE (*to the women*):
Help your mistress!

TRISTAN: O rapture filled with rancor!
O bliss that's blest by treach'ry!

ALLE MÄNNER *(Ausbruch allgemeinen Jauchzens)*:
       Kornwall Heil!
       (Trompeten vom Lande her.)
       (Leute sind über Bord gestiegen, andere
       haben eine Brücke ausgelegt, und die Halt-
       ung aller deutet auf die soeben bevorstehende
       Ankunft der Erwarteten, als der Vorhang
       schnell fällt.)

People have climbed aboard; others have rigged a gangway; their behavior indicates their expectation of the coming arrival.

ALL THE MEN: Cornwall, hail!

Trumpets are heard from the land.

CURTAIN

ZWEITER AUFZUG

Garten mit hohen Bäumen vor dem Gemach Isoldes, zu welchem, seitwärts gelegen, Stufen hinaufführen. Helle, anmutige Sommernacht. An der geöffneten Türe ist eine brennende Fackel aufgesteckt. — Jagdgetön. Brangäne, auf den Stufen am Gemach, späht dem immer entfernter vernehmbaren Jagdtrosse nach. Zu ihr tritt aus dem Gemach, feurig bewegt, Isolde.

ERSTER AUFTRITT

Isolde. Brangäne.

ISOLDE:
Hörst du sie noch?
Mir schwand schon fern der Klang.

BRANGÄNE *(lauschend)*:
Noch sind sie nah;
deutlich tönt's daher.

ISOLDE *(lauschend)*:
Sorgende Furcht
beirrt dein Ohr.
Dich täuscht des Laubes
säuselnd Getön',
das lachend schüttelt der Wind.

BRANGÄNE:
Dich täuscht des Wunsches
Ungestüm,
zu vernehmen, was du wähnst. *(Sie lauscht.)*
Ich höre der Hörner Schall.

ISOLDE *(wieder lauschend)*:
Nicht Hörnerschall
tönt so hold,
des Quelles sanft
rieselnde Welle
rauscht so wonnig daher.

ACT II

SCENE I

A garden with high trees before the chamber of Isolde, which lies at one side and is approached by steps. Bright and inviting summer night. A torch burns by the open door. A hunter's horn is heard. Brangaene, standing on the steps, is watching the retreating hunt, which can still be heard. She looks back into the chamber as Isolde emerges thence in ardent animation.

ISOLDE:
Can you still hear?
I've lost the distant sound.

BRANGAENE *(listening)*:
They are still near,
plainly to be heard.

Isolde listens.

ISOLDE:
Careful concern
deceives your ear.
You're fooled by rustling
sounds of the leaves,
that, laughing, shake in the wind.

BRANGAENE:
A wild desire
deludes your mind
to interpret as you please.
(She listens.)
I hear the resounding horns.

ISOLDE *(again listening)*:
No noise of horns
sounds so sweet;
the spring, with soft
purling of waters
runs so gaily along.

Wie hört' ich sie,
tosten noch Hörner?
Im Schweigen der Nacht
nur lacht mir der Quell.
Der meiner harrt
in schweigender Nacht,
als ob Hörner noch nah dir schallten,
willst du ihn fern mir halten?

BRANGÄNE: Der deiner harrt —
o hör mein Warnen! —
des harren Späher zur Nacht.
Weil du erblindet,
wähnst du den Blick
der Welt erblödet für euch?
Da dort an Schiffes Bord
von Tristans bebender Hand
die bleiche Braut,
kaum ihrer mächtig,
König Marke empfing,
als alles verwirrt
auf die Wankende sah,
der güt'ge König,
mild besorgt,
die Mühen der langen Fahrt,
die du littest, laut beklagt':
ein einz'ger war's,
ich achtet' es wohl,
der nur Tristan faßt' ins Auge.
Mit böslicher List
lauerndem Blick
sucht er in seiner Miene
zu finden, was ihm diene.
Tückisch lauschend
treff' ich ihn oft:
der heimlich euch umgarnt,
vor Melot seid gewarnt!

ISOLDE: Meinst du Herrn Melot?
O, wie du dich trügst!
Ist er nicht Tristans
treuester Freund?
Muß mein Trauter mich meiden,
dann weilt er bei Melot allein.

If horns still blared,
how could I hear this?
In stillness of night
I hear but the spring.
The one who waits
in the silence of night,
just because of fancied horn sounds,
would you prevent approaching?

BRANGAENE: The one who waits
—oh, hear my warning—
is now awaited by spies.
Being so blinded,
do you then think
the world is purblind to you?
That day, on board the ship,
from Tristan's hands, as they shook,
King Mark received
the pale and mightless,
sad and spiritless bride;
while all were confused,
as they gazed upon you,
the gracious sov'reign,
mild and kind,
expressed to you his concern
that your journey had been long:
but one there was
—I noted it well—
who fixed eyes on Tristan only;
with evil design
cunning in gaze,
well did he search his count'nance,
to find what there might serve him.
Oft I've seen his
eavesdropping ways:
he plans some secret snare;
of Melot, then, beware!

ISOLDE: Mean you Lord Melot?
Oh, how wrong you are!
Is he not Tristan's
truest of friends?
When my true love must shun me,
he tarries with Melot alone.

BRANGÄNE: Was mir ihn verdächtig,
      macht dir ihn teuer!
      Von Tristan zu Marke
      ist Melots Weg;
      dort sät er üble Saat.
      Die heut im Rat
      dies nächtliche Jagen
      so eilig schnell beschlossen,
      einem edlern Wild,
      als dein Wähnen meint,
      gilt ihre Jägerlist.

ISOLDE: Dem Freund zulieb'
      erfand diese List
      aus Mitleid
      Melot, der Freund.
      Nun willst du den Treuen schelten?
      Besser als du
      sorgt er für mich;
      ihm öffnet er,
      was mir du sperrst.
      O spare mir des Zögerns Not!
      Das Zeichen, Brangäne!
      O gib das Zeichen!
      Lösche des Lichtes
      letzten Schein!
      Daß ganz sie sich neige,
      winke der Nacht.
      Schon goß sie ihr Schweigen
      durch Hain und Haus,
      schon füllt sie das Herz
      mit wonnigem Graus.
      O lösche das Licht nun aus,
      lösche den scheuchenden Schein!
      Laß meinen Liebsten ein!

BRANGÄNE: O laß die warnende Zünde,
      laß die Gefahr sie dir zeigen!
      O wehe! Wehe!
      Ach mir Armen!
      Des unseligen Trankes!
      Daß ich untreu
      einmal nur
      der Herrin Willen trog!

BRANGAENE: My reason for doubting
is yours for loving!
From Tristan to sov'reign
is Melot's route;
he there sows evil seed.
And those who planned
this evening hunting
with hasty-quick arrangement
look for nobler game
than your fancy deems
worthy their hunters' skill.

ISOLDE: For Tristan's sake
the plan was devised,
for Melot
pities his friend.
And will you reproach him for that?
He cares for me
better than you;
he shows to him
what you have closed.
Oh, spare delay and all its woes!
The signal, Brangaene!
Oh, give the signal!
Out with the light's last
flickering spark.
That she may enwrap us,
beckon the night!
She's poured out her silence
on grove and house;
my heart has she filled
with rapturous awe.
Oh, now let the light be quenched!
Put out its frightening glare!
Let my beloved in!

BRANGAENE: The torch of warning should stay there.
Let it illumine your danger.
O sorrow, sorrow!
Ah, poor creature!
That most unblessed of potions!
That I just once
was unfaithful
to my mistress' will!

Gehorcht' ich taub und blind,
dein Werk
war dann der Tod.
Doch deine Schmach,
deine schmählichste Not
mein Werk,
muß ich Schuld'ge es wissen?

ISOLDE:

Dein Werk?
O tör'ge Magd!
Frau Minne kenntest du nicht?
Nicht ihres Zaubers Macht?
Des kühnsten Mutes
Königin?
Des Weltenwerdens
Walterin?
Leben und Tod
sind untertan ihr,
die sie webt aus Lust und Leid,
in Liebe wandelnd den Neid.
Des Todes Werk,
nahm ich's vermessen zur Hand,
Frau Minne hat es
meiner Macht entwandt.
Die Todgeweihte
nahm sie in Pfand,
faßte das Werk
in ihre Hand.
Wie sie es wendet,
wie sie es endet,
was sie mir küre,
wohin mich führe,
ihr ward ich zu eigen:
nun laß mich Gehorsam zeigen!

BRANGÄNE:

Und mußte der Minne
tückischer Trank
des Sinnes Licht dir verlöschen,
darfst du nicht sehen,
wenn ich dich warne:
nur heute hör,
o hör mein Flehen!
Der Gefahr leuchtendes Licht,
nur heute, heut
die Fackel dort lösche nicht!

Had I been deaf and blind,
your work
were then your death:
yet your disgrace,
your most shameful distress
I caused—
I am guilty, I own it!

ISOLDE: Your work?
O foolish maid!
Do you not know Lady Love,
nor know her magic pow'r?
The mighty queen of
valiant hearts
who rules all earthly
destiny?
Life and death
are subject to her,
these she weaves of joy and pain;
she changes hate into love.
The work of death
I boldly took into my hands,
Love's goddess, though, has
torn it from my pow'r.
The death-devoted
she took in pledge,
and seized the work
in her own hands.
Nor how she turns it,
nor how she ends it,
nor what she gives me,
nor where she leads me,
makes her less than own me:
so let me obey her orders!

BRANGAENE: And even if love's
insidious drink
puts out the light of your reason,
though you may see not,
now, when I warn you:
just hear me once,
Oh, hear my prayer!
Oh, beware: danger's awake!
Just once, this night
allow the torch, quench it not!

ISOLDE: Die im Busen mir
                     die Glut entfacht,
                     die mir das Herze
                     brennen macht,
                     die mir als Tag
                     der Seele lacht,
                     Frau Minne will:
                     es werde Nacht,
                     daß hell sie dorten leuchte,
                     (sie eilt auf die Fackel zu)
                     wo sie dein Licht verscheuchte.
                     (Sie nimmt die Fackel von der Tür.)
                     Zur Warte du:
                     dort wache treu!
                     Die Leuchte,
                     und wär's meines Lebens Licht —
                     lachend
                     sie zu löschen zag' ich nicht!
                     *(Sie wirft die Fackel zur Erde, wo sie
                     allmählich verlischt.)*
                     *(Brangäne wendet sich bestürzt ab, um auf
                     einer äußeren Treppe die Zinne zu ersteigen,
                     wo sie langsam verschwindet.)*
                     *(Isolde lauscht und späht, zunächst schüch-
                     tern, in einen Baumgang. Von wachsendem
                     Verlangen bewegt, schreitet sie dem Baum-
                     gang näher und späht zuversichtlicher. Sie
                     winkt mit einem Tuche, erst seltener, dann
                     häufiger, und endlich, in leidenschaftlicher
                     Ungeduld, immer schneller. Eine Gebärde
                     des plötzlichen Entzückens sagt, daß sie den
                     Freund in der Ferne gewahr geworden. Sie
                     streckt sich höher und höher, und, um besser
                     den Raum zu übersehen, eilt sie zur Treppe
                     zurück, von deren oberster Stufe aus sie dem
                     Herannahenden zuwinkt.)*

ISOLDE: She that fans the glow
                           within my breast,
                           she that has set my
                           heart on fire,
                           who smiles as day
                           upon my soul,
                           Love's goddess wills
                           it should be night,
                           that brightly she illumine
                           (She hastens toward the torch.)
                           the place where your light drove her.
                           (She takes the torch from the doorway.)
                           So go on guard:
                           and keep true watch!
                           The splendor
                           —though it were my light of life—
                           laughing,
                           without tremor I would quench!

*She throws the torch to the ground, where it
gradually goes out. Brangaene turns dis-
tressedly away in order to get upon the
parapet by an outer staircase, where she
slowly disappears. Isolde listens and looks,
at first timidly, down the avenue of trees.
Stirred by increasing longing, she goes nearer
to the avenue and looks out more boldly.
She waves her kerchief, at first from time
to time, then oftener, finally with passionate
impatience, faster and faster. A gesture of
sudden delight shows that she has perceived
her lover in the distance. She raises herself
higher and higher, the better to overlook the
place, then hurries back to the steps, from
the top of which she beckons to him as he
approaches.*

ZWEITER AUFTRITT

Tristan und Isolde.

TRISTAN *(stürzt herein)*:
  Isolde! Geliebte!

ISOLDE *(ihm entgegenspringend)*:
  Tristan! Geliebter!
  *(Stürmische Umarmungen beider, unter
  denen sie in den Vordergrund gelangen.)*
  Bist du mein?

TRISTAN: Hab' ich dich wieder?

ISOLDE: Darf ich dich fassen?

TRISTAN: Kann ich mir trauen?

ISOLDE: Endlich! Endlich!

TRISTAN: An meiner Brust!

ISOLDE: Fühl' ich dich wirklich?

TRISTAN: Seh' ich dich selber?

ISOLDE: Dies deine Augen?

TRISTAN: Dies dein Mund?

ISOLDE: Hier deine Hand?

TRISTAN: Hier dein Herz?

ISOLDE: Bin ich's? Bist du's?
  Halt' ich dich fest?

TRISTAN: Bin ich's? Bist du's?
  Ist es kein Trug?

BEIDE: Ist es kein Traum?
  O Wonne der Seele,
  o süße, hehrste,
  kühnste, schönste,
  seligste Lust!

Scene II

TRISTAN *(rushing in)*:

Isolde! Beloved!

ISOLDE:

Tristan! Beloved!

They embrace passionately, then come down to the front.

Are you mine?

TRISTAN:

Now do I have you?

ISOLDE:

Dare I embrace you?

TRISTAN:

Can I believe it?

ISOLDE:

No more waiting!

TRISTAN:

Come to my breast!

ISOLDE:

Now do I touch you?

TRISTAN:

Whom do I see here?

ISOLDE:

Are these your eyes?

TRISTAN:

This your mouth?

ISOLDE:

Is this your hand?

TRISTAN:

Here your heart?

ISOLDE:

Is it I? Is't you
here in my arms?

TRISTAN:

Is it I? Is't you?
Is it no trick?

BOTH:

Is it no dream?
Glorious rapture!
O sweetest, highest,
keenest, fairest,
blessedest joy!

TRISTAN:	Ohne Gleiche!
ISOLDE:	Überreiche!
TRISTAN:	Überselig!
ISOLDE:	Ewig!
TRISTAN:	Ewig!
ISOLDE:	Ungeahnte, nie gekannte!
TRISTAN:	Überschwenglich hoch erhabne!
ISOLDE:	Freudejauchzen!
TRISTAN:	Lustentzücken!
BEIDE:	Himmelhöchstes Weltentrücken! Mein! { Tristan / Isolde } mein! Mein und dein! Ewig, ewig ein!
ISOLDE:	Wie lange fern! Wie fern so lang!
TRISTAN:	Wie weit so nah! So nah wie weit!
ISOLDE:	O Freundesfeindin, böse Ferne! Träger Zeiten zögernde Länge!
TRISTAN:	O Weit' und Nähe, hart entzweite! Holde Nähe! Öde Weite!
ISOLDE:	Im Dunkel du, im Lichte ich!
TRISTAN:	Das Licht! Das Licht! O dieses Licht, wie lang verlosch es nicht!

TRISTAN:	Without equal!
ISOLDE:	Beyond riches!
TRISTAN:	More than blessed!
ISOLDE:	Endless!
TRISTAN:	Endless!
ISOLDE:	Never dreamed of! Never known of!
TRISTAN:	Exaltation never equaled!
ISOLDE:	Joy-exulting!
TRISTAN:	Raptured pleasure!
BOTH:	Heaven-high above all earthly! Mine! { Tristan! / Isolde! } Mine! Mine and yours! Ever, ever one!
ISOLDE:	How long afar! How far so long!
TRISTAN:	So far, yet near! So near, yet far!
ISOLDE:	O foe to friendship, wicked distance! Slothful hours of tedious slowness!
TRISTAN:	But far, or near you, hard division! Precious nearness! Barren distance!
ISOLDE:	The dark for you, the light for me!
TRISTAN:	The light! The light! O troubling light, how long before it's out?

Die Sonne sank,
der Tag verging,
doch seinen Neid
erstickt' er nicht:
sein scheuchend Zeichen
zündet er an
und steckt's an der Liebsten Türe,
daß nicht ich zu ihr führe,

ISOLDE: Doch der Liebsten Hand
löschte das Licht;
wes die Magd sich wehrte,
scheut' ich mich nicht:
in Frau Minnes Macht und Schutz
bot ich dem Tage Trutz!

TRISTAN: Dem Tage! Dem Tage!
Dem tückischen Tage,
dem härtesten Feinde
Haß und Klage!
Wie du das Licht,
o könnt' ich die Leuchte,
der Liebe Leiden zu rächen,
dem frechen Tage verlöschen!
Gibt's eine Not,
gibt's eine Pein,
die er nicht weckt
mit seinem Schein?
Selbst in der Nacht
dämmernder Pracht
hegt ihn Liebchen am Haus,
streckt mir drohend ihn aus!

ISOLDE: Hegt ihn die Liebste
am eignen Haus,
im eignen Herzen
hell und kraus
hegt' ihn trotzig
einst mein Trauter:
Tristan — der mich betrog!
War's nicht der Tag,
der aus ihm log,
als er nach Irland
werbend zog,

The sun has sunk,
the day has fled,
yet out of spite
the light remains:
it lights a fearful
sign which it set
beside my beloved's doorway,
so that I may not reach her.

ISOLDE:

Yet the loved one's hand
smothered the light;
what my handmaid turned from,
I did not fear.
Through love's guarding care and might
I here defy the day!

TRISTAN:

The daylight! The daylight!
To treacherous daylight,
my bitterest foe,
laments and loathing!
As you the light,
Oh, could I extinguish
the lording day with its beacons,
thus venging love for its suff'rings!
Is there one woe,
is there one pain
that is not wakened
by its glare?
Even in night's
splendor of dusk,
first she took in this bane,
then she proffered it me.

ISOLDE:

What if I took in
the baneful light,
defiantly my
loved one harbored
this light within
his bosom—
Tristan, who tricked his love!
Was't not the day
that lied through him
when he sought Ireland
for his king,

für Marke mich zu frein,
dem Tod die Treue zu weihn?

TRISTAN: Der Tag! Der Tag,
der dich umgliß,
dahin, wo sie
der Sonne glich,
in höchster Ehren
Glanz und Licht
Isolde mir entrückt'!
Was mir das Auge
so entzückt',
mein Herze tief
zur Erde drückt':
in lichten Tages Schein
wie war Isolde mein?

ISOLDE: War sie nicht dein,
die dich erkor?
Was log der böse
Tag dir vor,
daß, die für dich beschieden,
die Traute du verrietest?

TRISTAN: Was dich umgliß
mit hehrster Pracht,
der Ehre Glanz,
des Ruhmes Macht,
an sie mein Herz zu hangen,
hielt mich der Wahn gefangen.
Die mit des Schimmers
hellstem Schein
mir Haupt und Scheitel
licht beschien,
der Welten-Ehren
Tagessonne,
mit ihrer Strahlen
eitler Wonne,
durch Haupt und Scheitel
drang mir ein
bis in des Herzens
tiefsten Schrein.
Was dort in keuscher Nacht
dunkel verschlossen wacht',

and I was wooed for Mark
that thus the true one might die?

TRISTAN: The day! The day
has made you glow
and shine splendid
in honor's light,
but infinitely
far removed,
just like the sun itself!
The sight that so
entranced my eye,
weighed down my heart
to earthy depths:
in brilliant light of day,
how could Isold' be mine?

ISOLDE: Was she not yours
who called you hers?
What lies did wicked
day devise
that made you trick the true one
who chose you as her loved one?

TRISTAN: A splendid aura
gave you grace:
your honor's light,
your high renown,
to make my heart a captive—
these seized my ardent fancy.
These with their brilliant
rays of light
shone lightly on my
head and crown;
but day's bright sun of
worldly honor
with its resplendent,
empty rapture
pierced strongly through my
crown and head
down to my heart's most
hidden shrine.
The chaste night held it there,
where, locked in dark, it woke,

was ohne Wiss' und Wahn
ich dämmernd dort empfahn:
ein Bild, das meine Augen
zu sehn sich nicht getrauten,
von des Tages Schein betroffen
lag mir's da schimmernd offen.
Was mir so rühmlich
schien und hehr,
das rühmt' ich hell
vor allem Heer;
vor allem Volke
pries ich laut
der Erde schönste
Königsbraut.
Dem Neid, den mir
der Tag erweckt';
dem Eifer, den
mein Glücke schreckt';
der Mißgunst, die mir Ehren
und Ruhm begann zu schweren:
denen bot ich Trotz,
und treu beschloß,
um Ehr' und Ruhm zu wahren,
nach Irland ich zu fahren.

ISOLDE: O eitler Tagesknecht!
Getäuscht von ihm,
der dich getäuscht,
wie mußt' ich liebend
um dich leiden,
den, in des Tages
falschem Prangen,
von seines Gleißens
Trug befangen,
dort, wo ihn Liebe
heiß umfaßte,
im tiefsten Herzen
hell ich haßte.
Ach, in des Herzens Grunde
wie schmerzte tief die Wunde!
Den dort ich heimlich barg,
wie dünkt' er mich so arg,
wenn in des Tages Scheine

this thing I had not dreamed,
just dimly had perceived,
a picture that my eyes did not
dare so much as gaze on,
when a ray of day revealed it,
and made it shine before me.
What seemed so
glorious-sublime
I lauded forth to
all the host;
to all the folk I
cried your praise
as bride on earth most
fit for kings.
The spite—the envy
waked by day;
the passion that
my luck dismayed—
the ill-will that began to
oppress my fame and honor,
I defied them all,
and undertook
to save that fame and honor
by faring back to Ireland.

ISOLDE: O idle slave of day!
Deceived by it,
deceived, like you,
how I have loved you
and so suffered,
whom, in the day's
deceitful splendor,
enthralled and
caught in glitt'ring fetters,
there, where a fiery
love embraced you,
within my hottest
heart I hated!
Ah, in my bosom's center,
how deep the wound was smarting!
the one there concealed,
how wicked did he seem
when in the day's effulgence

die treu gehegte Eine
der Liebe Blicken schwand,
als Feind nur vor mir stand!
Das als Verräter
dich mir wies,
dem Licht des Tages
wollt' ich entfliehn,
dorthin in die Nacht
dich mit mir ziehn,
wo der Täuschung Ende
mein Herz mir verhieß;
wo des Trugs geahnter
Wahn zerrinne;
dort dir zu trinken
ew'ge Minne,
mit mir dich in Verein
wollt' ich dem Tode weihn.

TRISTAN: In deiner Hand
den süßen Tod,
als ich ihn erkannt,
den sie mir bot;
als mir die Ahnung
hehr und gewiß
zeigte, was mir
die Sühne verhieß:
da erdämmerte mild
erhabner Macht
im Busen mir die Nacht;
mein Tag war da vollbracht.

ISOLDE: Doch ach, dich täuschte
der falsche Trank,
daß dir von neuem
die Nacht versank;
dem einzig am Tode lag,
den gab er wieder dem Tag!

TRISTAN: O Heil dem Tranke!
Heil seinem Saft!
Heil seines Zaubers
hehrer Kraft!
Durch des Todes Tor,
wo er mir floß,

the one so truly cherished
had lost his loving look,
the foe, only, remained!
That which had showed you
false to me,
the light of day,
I now wished to flee,
and deep into night
draw you with me,
where my heart foretold me
the error would end;
where all feared deceit and
fraud would vanish,
there would I drink to you
love eternal.
I wished, joined into one,
we might be pledged in death.

TRISTAN: The time when I
did recognize
the sweet death you proffered
in the cup,
when intuition
surely and well
showed what the peace
pledge promised my hope:
then there came as a dawn
within my bosom,
mild, exalted night.
My day was then fulfilled.

ISOLDE: But ah, that false drink
deceived you too,
so that your night
vanished once again:
and one at the door of death
was brought again to the day!

TRISTAN: All hail the potion!
Hail to its juice!
Hail to its lofty
magical might!
Through the door of death,
where I quaffed it,

weit und offen
er mir erschloß,
darin ich sonst nur träumend gewacht,
das Wunderreich der Nacht.
Von dem Bild in des Herzens
bergendem Schrein
scheucht' er des Tages
täuschenden Schein,
daß nachtsichtig mein Auge
wahr es zu sehen tauge.

ISOLDE:

Doch es rächte sich
der verscheuchte Tag;
mit deinen Sünden
Rat's er pflag:
was dir gezeigt
die dämmernde Nacht,
an des Tag-Gestirnes
Königsmacht
mußtest du's übergeben,
um einsam
in öder Pracht
schimmernd dort zu leben.
Wie ertrug ich's nur?
Wie ertrag' ich's noch?

TRISTAN:

O, nun waren wir
Nacht-Geweihte!
Der tückische Tag,
der Neid-bereite,
trennen konnt' uns sein Trug,
doch nicht mehr täuschen sein Lug!
Seine eitle Pracht,
seinen prahlenden Schein
verlacht, wem die Nacht
den Blick geweiht:
seines flackernden Lichtes
flüchtige Blitze
blenden uns nicht mehr.
Wer des Todes Nacht
liebend erschaut,
wem sie ihr tief'
Geheimnis vertraut:
des Tages Lügen,

wide it opened
its wondrous realm,
wherein I'd wandered only in dreams,
the wonderland of night.
From the picture within my
heart's secret shrine,
gone was the lying
glitter of day:
my eyes, used to the darkness
now could perceive it truly.

ISOLDE: But affrighted day
took its due revenge,
and with your sins it
joined in league:
what you were shown
in shadowing night,
to the kingly might of
day's bright star,
you were forced to surrender,
and there now
it lives in lone,
lovely, barren splendor.
How have I borne this?
Can I bear it still?

TRISTAN: Oh, now we are night
consecrated!
Malevolent day,
disposed to envy,
though it part us through fraud
can trick us no more by lies!
All its idle pomp,
its braggardly show
is scorned by the man
with eyes night-blessed:
and the fugitive flashes
cast by its lightning
blind our eyes no more.
He who finds death's night
dear to his view,
he who has plumbed
the secrets and depths,
will hold day's falsehood,

Ruhm und Ehr',
Macht und Gewinn,
so schimmernd hehr,
wie eitler Staub der Sonnen
sind sie vor dem zersponnen!
In des Tages eitlem Wähnen
bleibt ihm ein einzig Sehnen —
das Sehnen hin
zur heil'gen Nacht,
wo ur-ewig,
einzig wahr
Liebeswonne ihm lacht!
*(Tristan zieht Isolde sanft zur Seite auf eine
Blumenbank nieder, senkt sich vor ihr auf
die Knie und schmiegt sein Haupt in ihren
Arm.)*

BEIDE: O sink hernieder,
              Nacht der Liebe,
              gib Vergessen,
              daß ich lebe;
              nimm mich auf
              in deinen Schoß,
              löse von
              der Welt mich los!

TRISTAN: Verloschen nun
              die letzte Leuchte;

ISOLDE: was wir dachten,
              was uns deuchte;

TRISTAN: all Gedenken —

ISOLDE: all Gemahnen —

BEIDE: heil'ger Dämm'rung
              hehres Ahnen
              löscht des Wähnens Graus
              welterlösend aus.

ISOLDE: Barg im busen
              uns sich die Sonne,
              leuchten lachend
              Sterne der Wonne.

fame and name,
honor and gain
—though dazzling bright—
as idle motes in sunlight,
which drift away and vanish.
Mid the daylight's idle fancies
he has one only longing,
a longing for
the holy night,
where forever,
solely true,
love and rapture await!
*(Tristan draws Isolde gently down on a
flowery bank at one side, sinks on his knees
before her and rests his head on her arm.)*

BOTH: Oh, close around us,
night of rapture,
grant forgetting,
that I'm living,
take me up,
unto your breast;
set me free
now from the world!

TRISTAN: Extinguished is
the light's last lantern.

ISOLDE: All our thinking,
all appearance.

TRISTAN: All remembrance.

ISOLDE: All recalling.

BOTH: Holy twilight's
lofty visions
make vain terrors melt,
setting spirit free.

ISOLDE: When the sun lies
hid in our bosoms,
laughing stars shine
forth in their rapture.

TRISTAN: Von deinem Zauber
                sanft umsponnen,
                vor deinen Augen
                süß zerronnen;

ISOLDE: Herz an Herz dir,
                Mund an Mund;

TRISTAN: eines Atems
                ein'ger Bund;

BEIDE: bricht mein Blick sich
                wonnerblindet.
                erbleicht die Welt
                mit ihrem Blenden:

ISOLDE: die uns der Tag
                trügend erhellt,

TRISTAN: zu täuschendem Wahn
                entgegengestellt,

BEIDE: selbst dann
                bin ich die Welt:
                Wonne-hehrstes Weben,
                Leibe-heiligstes Leben,
                Nie-wieder-Erwachens
                wahnlos
                hold bewußter Wunsch.
                (Tristan und Isolde versinken wie in gänz-
                liche Entrücktheit, in der sie, Haupt an
                Haupt auf die Blumenbank zurückgelehnt,
                verweilen.)

BRANGÄNES STIMME *(von der Zinne her):*
                Einsam wachend
                in der Nacht,
                wem der Traum
                der Liebe lacht,
                hab' der Einen
                Ruf in acht,
                die den Schläfern
                Schlimmes ahnt,
                bange zum
                Erwachen mahnt.
                Habet acht!
                Habet acht!
                Bald entweicht die Nacht

TRISTAN: Your gentle magic
flows about us,
before your eyes
so sweetly swooning.

ISOLDE: Heart on heart and
mouth on mouth.

TRISTAN: Merged in one, in
one sole breath.

BOTH: Eyes are dazed by
blinding rapture,
earth pales away
with all its glitter.

ISOLDE: Giv'n by the day
just to mislead.

TRISTAN: All earthly illusion
here I defy:

BOTH: I myself
am the world.
Joy that weaves our rapture,
Life of love at its holiest,
no more reawak'ning,
dreamless,
sweet, awaited wish.
*(Completely carried away, Tristan and Isolde
sink down and remain lying on the flowery
bank, their heads side by side.)*

BRANGAENE *(from the turret, invisible):*
While I watch
alone by night:
you who bask
in dreams of love,
give my only
cry your heed,
for it warns of
woe to come.
Oh, beware,
I urge you wake!
Have a care!
Soon the night will fade!

ISOLDE *(leise)*:   Lausch, Geliebter!

TRISTAN *(ebenso)*:Laß mich sterben!

ISOLDE *(allmählich sich ein wenig erhebend)*:
                 Neid'sche Wache!

TRISTAN *(zurückgelehnt bleibend)*:
                 Nie erwachen!

ISOLDE: Doch der Tag
                 muß Tristan wecken?

TRISTAN *(ein wenig das Haupt erhebend)*:
                 Laß den Tag
                 dem Tode weichen!

ISOLDE: Tag und Tod
                 mit gleichen Streichen
                 sollten unsre
                 Lieb' erreichen?

TRISTAN *(sich mehr aufrichtend)*:
                 Unsre Liebe?
                 Tristans Liebe?
                 Dein' und mein',
                 Isoldes Liebe?
                 Welches Todes Streichen
                 könnte je sie weichen?
                 Stünd' er vor mir,
                 der mächt'ge Tod,
                 wie er mir Leib
                 und Leben bedroht',
                 die ich so willig
                 die Liebe lasse,
                 wie wäre seinen Streichen
                 die Liebe selbst zu erreichen?
                 *(Immer inniger mit dem Haupt sich an Isolde
                 schmiegend.)*
                 Stürb' ich nun ihr,
                 der so gern ich sterbe,
                 wie könnte die Liebe
                 mit mir sterben,
                 die ewig lebende
                 mit mir enden?

ISOLDE: Hark, beloved!

TRISTAN: Let me die now!

ISOLDE (*gently raising herself a little*):
Envious watcher!

TRISTAN: No more waking!

ISOLDE: Must the day
not waken Tristan?

TRISTAN (*raising his head a little*):
Let the day
to death be given!

ISOLDE: Would not day
and death as equals
overtake our
love and rend it?

TRISTAN (*raising himself slightly*):
Love as ours is?
Tristan's passion?
Yours and mine,
Isolde's passion?
Even though Death lashed it,
could it ever weaken?
Were mighty Death
to stand here now,
threatening both
my life and my limbs,
trying to will me
to love no longer,
how could he ever hope to
destroy the love that I harbor?
Dying for that I'd so gladly die for,
how could such a love then
die when I do,
how could the endlessly
living perish?

Doch stürbe nie seine Liebe,
wie stürbe dann Tristan
seiner Liebe?

ISOLDE·   Doch unsre Liebe,
heißt sie nicht Tristan
und — Isolde?
Dies süße Wörtlein: und,
was es bindet,
der Liebe Bund,
wenn Tristan stürb',
zerstört' es nicht der Tod?

TRISTAN: Was stürbe dem Tod,
als was uns stört,
was Tristan wehrt,
Isolde immer zu lieben,
ewig ihr nur zu leben?

ISOLDE: Doch dieses Wörtlein: und —
wär' es zerstört,
wie anders als
mit Isoldes eignem Leben
wär' Tristan der Tod gegeben?
(Tristan zieht, mit bedeutungsvoller Gebärde,
Isolde sanft an sich.)

TRISTAN: So stürben wir,
um ungetrennt,
ewig einig
ohne End',
ohn' Erwachen,
ohn' Erbangen,
namenlos
in Lieb' umfangen,
ganz uns selbst gegeben,
der Liebe nur zu leben!

ISOLDE *(wie in sinnender Entrücktheit zu ihm aufblickend):*
So stürben wir,
um ungetrennt —

TRISTAN: ewig einig
ohne End' —

ISOLDE: ohn' Erwachen —

Yet if his love could not perish,
could Tristan die yoked to
love eternal?

ISOLDE: Yet, may we name it,
this love, as Tristan
and Isolde?
This little, sweet word "and":
how it binds us
—this bond of love—
if Tristan died
would death not murder this?

TRISTAN: What could death destroy
but what prevents
your Tristan's heart
from ever loving his Isold',
ever living for Isold'?

ISOLDE: Yet, how to cancel this
little word "and":
how otherwise than
with Isold's very life were
death to be given Tristan?

*Tristan, with expressive gestures, draws
Isolde gently to him.*

TRISTAN: But should we die,
we would not part,
joined forever,
without end,
never waking,
never fearing,
nameless there,
in love enfolded,
each to each belonging,
with love alone our life source!

ISOLDE *(looking up at him in thoughtful absorption)*:
But should we die,
we would not part . . .

TRISTAN: joined forever,
without end . . .

ISOLDE: never waking . . .

TRISTAN: ohn' Erbangen —

BEIDE: namenlos
                      in Lieb' umfangen
                      ganz uns selbst gegeben,
                      der Liebe nur zu leben!
                      *(Isolde neigt wie überwältigt das Haupt an
                      seine Brust.)*

BRANGÄNES STIMME *(wie vorher)*:
                      Habet acht!
                      Habet acht!
                      Schon weicht dem Tag die Nacht.

TRISTAN *(lächelnd zu Isolde geneigt)*:
                      Soll ich lauschen?

ISOLDE *(schwärmerisch zu Tristan aufblickend)*:
                      Laß mich sterben!

TRISTAN *(ernster)*:
                      Muß ich wachen?

ISOLDE *(bewegter)*:
                      Nie erwachen!

TRISTAN *(drängender)*:
                      Soll der Tag
                      noch Tristan wecken?

ISOLDE *(begeistert)*:
                      Laß den Tag
                      dem Tode weichen!

TRISTAN: Des Tages Dräuen
                      nun trotzten wir so?

ISOLDE *(mit wachsender Begeisterung)*:
                      Seinem Trug ewig zu fliehn.

TRISTAN: Sein dämmernder Schein
                      verscheuchte uns nie?

ISOLDE *(mit großer Gebärde ganz sich erhebend)*:
                      Ewig währ' uns die Nacht!
                      *(Tristan folgt ihr, sie umfangen sich in
                      schwärmerischer Begeisterung.)*

TRISTAN: never fearing . . .

BOTH: nameless there,
in love enfolded,
each to each belonging,
with love alone our life source!

Isolde, as if overpowered, droops her head upon his breast.

BRANGAENE'S VOICE *(as before)*:
Have a care!
Have a care!
The night gives place to day!

TRISTAN *(bends smilingly down to Isolde)*:
Shall I listen?

ISOLDE *(gazing fondly at Tristan)*:
Let me die thus!

TRISTAN *(more gravely)*:
Must I waken?

ISOLDE *(more affected)*:
Never waken!

TRISTAN: Must the day
yet waken Tristan?

BOTH: Let the day
to death surrender!

TRISTAN: But shall we now give
defiance to day?

ISOLDE *(with rising ecstasy)*:
Could we fly far from its fraud!

TRISTAN: The light of its dawn would never bring fear.

ISOLDE *(rising to her feet)*:
Let the night never end!

Tristan follows her; they embrace in a fond ecstasy.

BEIDE: O ew'ge Nacht,
süße Nacht!
Hehr erhabne
Liebesnacht!
Wen du umfangen,
wem du gelacht,
wie wär' ohne Bangen
aus dir er je erwacht?
Nun banne das Bangen,
holder Tod,
sehnend verlangter
Liebestod!
In deinen Armen,
dir geweiht,
ur-heilig Erwarmen,
von Erwachens Not befreit!

TRISTAN: Wie sie fassen,
wie sie lassen,
diese Wonne —

BEIDE: Fern der Sonne,
fern der Tage
Trennungsklage!

ISOLDE: Ohne Wähnen —

TRISTAN: sanftes Sehnen;

ISOLDE: ohne Bangen —

TRISTAN: süß Verlangen.
Ohne Wehen —

BEIDE: hehr Vergehen.

ISOLDE: Ohne Schmachten —

BEIDE: hold Umnachten.

TRISTAN: Ohne Meiden —

BEIDE: ohne Scheiden,
traut allein,
ewig heim,
in ungemeßnen Räumen
übersel'ges Träumen.

BOTH:	O endless night, blissful night! noble-lofty night of love! Those whom you compass, those whom you love, could they without dismay waken from your sleep? Let fear now be banished, gracious death, yearningly longed-for love-in-death. Within your arms we are yours, warmth, prime and most holy, from awakening's woes set free!
TRISTAN:	How to grasp it, how to lose it. This enchantment . . .
ISOLDE:	Far from sunlight, far from daylight's parting outcries! No illusions, . . .
TRISTAN:	. . . tender yearnings!
ISOLDE:	All fear ended, . . .
TRISTAN:	. . . sweet desiring! No more sorrow, . . .
BOTH:	Noble surcease!
ISOLDE:	No more pining . . .
BOTH:	. . . night-encompassed.
TRISTAN:	No more parting . . .
BOTH:	. . . no more sundered, yet alone, always home, in realms of endless grandeur, dream of blessed wonder!

TRISTAN: Tristan du,
                   ich Isolde,
                   nicht mehr Tristan!

ISOLDE: Du Isolde,
                   Tristan ich,
                   nicht mehr Isolde!

BEIDE: Ohne Nennen,
                   ohne Trennen,
                   neu' Erkennen,
                   neu' Entbrennen;
                   ewig endlos,
                   ein-bewußt:
                   heiß erglühter Brust
                   höchste Liebeslust!
                   (Sie bleiben in verzückter Stellung.)
                   (Brangäne stößt einen grellen Schrei aus.)
                   *(Kurwenal stürzt mit entblößtem Schwerte
                   herein.)*

ISOLDE: You Isolde . . .

TRISTAN: . . . you Tristan!

ISOLDE: Tristan I, . . .

TRISTAN: . . . I Isolde!

ISOLDE: No more Isolde!

TRISTAN: No more Tristan!

BOTH: No more naming,
             no more parting,
             newborn knowledge,
             newborn ardors,
             ever endless,
             both one mind:
             hotly glowing breast,
             love's supreme delight!

             They keep their positions, as if entranced.
             Brangaene utters a piercing shriek, as Kur-
             venal enters with drawn sword.

Dritter Auftritt

*Die Vorigen. Kurwenal, Brangäne, Marke, Melot und
Hofleute.*

KURWENAL: Rette dich, Tristan!
                *(Er blickt mit Entsetzen hinter sich in die
                Szene zurück. Marke, Melot und Hofleute,
                in Jägertracht, kommen aus dem Baumgange
                lebhaft nach dem Vordergrunde und halten
                entsetzt der Gruppe der Liebenden gegen-
                über an. Brangäne kommt zuleich von der
                Zinne herab und stürzt auf Isolde zu. Diese,
                von unwillkürlicher Scham ergriffen, lehnt
                sich, mit abgewandtem Gesicht, auf die
                Blumenbank. Tristan, in ebenfalls unwill-
                kürlicher Bewegung, streckt mit dem einen
                Arm den Mantel breit aus, so daß er Isolde
                vor den Blicken der Ankommenden verdeckt.
                In dieser Stellung verbleibt er längere Zeit,
                unbeweglich den starren Blick auf die Män-
                ner gerichtet, die in verschiedener Bewegung
                die Augen auf ihn heften. Morgendämmer-
                ung.)*

TRISTAN *(nach längerem Schweigen)*:
                Der öde Tag
                zum letztenmal!

MELOT *(zu Marke)*:
                Das sollst du, Herr, mir sagen,
                ob ich ihn recht verklagt?
                Das dir zum Pfand ich gab,
                ob ich mein Haupt gewahrt?
                Ich zeigt' ihn dir
                in offner Tat:
                Namen und Ehr'
                hab' ich getreu
                vor Schande dir bewahrt.

SCENE III

KURVENAL: Save yourself, Tristan!

*He looks off stage behind him in great alarm.
Mark, Melot, and courtiers, in hunting dress,
come quickly from the avenue toward the
front, and pause in amazement before the
lovers. In the meantime Brangaene descends
from the turret and rushes toward Isolde,
who, with instinctive shame, leans with
averted face upon the flowery bank. Tristan,
with an equally instinctive movement, with
one arm spreads his cloak so as to conceal
Isolde from the eyes of the newcomers. In
this position he remains for some time, his
eyes steadily fixed upon the men who look
at him with varied emotions. Morning dawns.*

TRISTAN: This dreary day,
                 last time of all!

MELOT *(to Mark)*:
                 Now will you, Lord, please tell me
                 if I accused aright?
                 and what I staked as pledge,
                 my head, is it still mine?
                 I've shown him in
                 the very act.
                 Well did I watch,
                 saving your honored
                 name and fame from shame.

MARKE *(nach tiefer Erschütterung, mit bebender Stimme)*:
          Tatest du's wirklich?
          Wähnst du das?
          Sieh ihn dort,
          den treusten aller Treuen;
          blick' auf ihn,
          den freundlichsten der Freunde:
          seiner Treue
          freiste Tat
          traf mein Herz
          mit feindlichstem Verrat!
          Trog mich Tristan,
          sollt' ich hoffen,
          was sein Trügen
          mir getroffen,
          sei durch Melots Rat
          redlich mir bewahrt?

TRISTAN *(krampfhaft heftig)*:
          Tagsgespenster!
          Morgenträume!
          Täuschend und wüst!
          Entschwebt! Entweicht!

MARKE *(mit tiefer Ergriffenheit)*:
          Mir dies?
          Dies, Tristan, mir? —
          Wohin nun Treue,
          da Tristan mich betrog?
          Wohin nun Ehr'
          und echte Art,
          da aller Ehren Hort,
          da Tristan sie verlor?
          Die Tristan sich
          zum Schild erkor,
          wohin ist Tugend
          nun entflohn,
          da meinen Freund sie flieht,
          da Tristan mich verriet?
          (Tristan senkt langsam den Blick zu Boden;
          in seinen Mienen ist, während Marke fort-
          fährt, zunehmende Trauer zu lesen.)
          Wozu die Dienste
          ohne Zahl,

MARK *(violently affected, then with trembling voice)*:

Have you though, really?
Is it true?
See him there,
the truest of all true ones;
look on him,
the best of friends in friendship:
yet his best, his
freest deed
was to stab
my heart by playing false!
If he tricked me,
shall I hope then
what his treachery had ruined
might through Melot be
somehow truly saved?

TRISTAN:

Daytime phantoms!
Morning dream-stuff!
Lying and vain!
Disperse! Dissolve!

MARK *(in sorrowful reproach)*:

You, though!
This, Tristan, to me?
Where then is truth found,
if Tristan has betrayed?
Where are good faith
and honor gone,
when he who was their guard,
my Tristan, lost them all?
And what he chose
himself for shield,
his virtue, now, where
has it flown,
since it has fled my friend,
my Tristan, who betrayed?

Tristan slowly drops his eyes to the ground; his face expresses his increasing sorrow as Mark continues.

Whereto your services
untold,

der Ehren Ruhm,
der Größe, Macht,
die Marken du gewannst;
mußt' Ehr' und Ruhm,
Größ' und Macht,
mußte die Dienste
ohne Zahl
dir Markes Schmach bezahlen?
Dünkte zu wenig
dich sein Dank,
daß, was du ihm erworben,
Ruhm und Reich,
er zu Erb' und Eigen dir gab?
Da kinderlos einst
schwand sein Weib,
so liebt' er dich,
daß nie aufs neu'
sich Marke wollt' vermählen.
Da alles Volk
zu Hof und Land
mit Bitt' und Dräuen
in ihn drang,
die Königin dem Lande,
die Gattin sich zu kiesen;
da selber du
den Ohm beschworst,
des Hofes Wunsch,
des Landes Willen
gütlich zu erfüllen;
in Wehr wider Hof und Land,
in Wehr selbst gegen dich,
mit List und Güte
weigerte er sich,
bis, Tristan, du ihm drohtest,
für immer zu meiden
Hof und Land,
würdest du selber
nicht entsandt,
dem König die Braut zu frein.
Da ließ er's denn so sein. —
Dies wundervolle Weib,
das mir dein Mut gewann,
wer durft' es sehen,

that honor, fame,
and puissant might
you won for Mark, your king;
if honor, fame,
puissant might,
if all your services untold
be paid with Mark's dishonor?
Thought you so little
of his thanks,
that when you gained and gave him
fame and kingdom
he made you heir to it all?
When childless he lost
once his wife,
he loved you so,
that he would never
wish a second marriage.
When all his folk
in court and land
pressed on him breathing
prayers and threats,
that he should help his country
and choose himself a consort;
when you yourself
urged on your king
the court's desire,
the country's wishes,
graciously be granted:
opposed to the court and land,
opposed to you yourself,
with tact and kindness
did he not decline,
till, Tristan, you did threaten
for ever to leave
the court and land,
if you yourself
were not dispatched
to woo for the king a bride?
He let it be that way.
This woman nonpareiled
your daring won for me,
who could behold her,

wer es kennen,
wer mit Stolze
sein es nennen,
ohne selig sich zu preisen?
Der mein Wille
nie zu nahen wagte,
der mein Wunsch
ehrfurchtscheu entsagte,
die so herrlich
hold erhaben
mir die Seele
mußte laben,
trotz Feind und Gefahr,
die fürstliche Braut
brachtest du mir dar.
Nun, da durch solchen
Besitz mein Herz
du fühlsamer schufst
als sonst dem Schmerz,
dort, wo am weichsten,
zart und offen,
würd' ich getroffen,
nie zu hoffen,
daß je ich könnte gesunden:
warum so sehrend,
Unseliger,
dort nun mich verwunden?
Dort mit der Waffe
quälendem Gift,
das Sinn und Hirn
mir sengend versehrt,
das mir dem Freund
die Treue verwehrt,
mein offnes Herz
erfüllt mit Verdacht,
daß ich nun heimlich
in dunkler Nacht
den Freund lauschend beschleiche,
meiner Ehren Ende erreiche?
Die kein Himmel erlöst,
warum mir diese Hölle?
Die kein Elend sühnt,
warum mir diese Schmach?

who could know her,
who so proudly
say he owned her
and not count himself most blessed?
Whom my will had
never dared to reach to,
whom my wish
feared to make a claim to,
whom, so nobly
good and gracious,
truly would
inspire my spirit;
'gainst foes and alarms,
a bride for a prince,
her you brought to me.
Now, when through such a
possession I
was more than before
aware of pain,
there where the wound
shows sore and open,
there have you struck me,
nevermore with
a hope to really recover,
why was I wounded
so terribly,
there, O most unblest one?
There with your poisoned
weapon so pierced,
that sense and brain
are scorched and burned,
destroying faith
in friend that was true,
and filling
frankest heart with distrust,
that I now covertly
dog my friend
by night, listening and spying,
bringing disrepute to my honor.
Why such hell to endure
which no heaven can save from?
Why this shameful blot
no suff'ring can atone?

Den unerforschlich tief
geheimnisvollen Grund,
wer macht der Welt ihn kund?

TRISTAN *(mitleidig das Auge zu Marke erhebend):*
O König, das
kann ich dir nicht sagen;
und was du frägst,
das kannst du nie erfahren.
*(Er wendet sich zu Isolde, die sehnsüchtig
zu ihm aufblickt.)*
Wohin nun Tristan scheidet,
willst du, Isold', ihm folgen?
Dem Land, das Tristan meint,
der Sonne Licht nicht scheint:
es ist das dunkel
nächt'ge Land,
daraus die Mutter
mich entsandt,
als, den im Tode
sie empfangen,
im Tod sie ließ
an das Licht gelangen.
Was, da sie mich gebar,
ihr Liebesberge war,
das Wunderreich der Nacht,
aus der ich einst erwacht:
das bietet dir Tristan,
dahin geht er voran:
ob sie ihm folge
treu und hold —
das sag ihm nun Isold'!

ISOLDE:
Als für ein fremdes Land
der Freund sie einstens warb,
dem Unholden
treu und hold
mußt' Isolde folgen.
Nun führst du in Eigen,
dein Erbe mir zu zeigen;
wie flöh ich wohl das Land,
das alle Welt umspannt?
Wo Tristans Haus und Heim,
da kehr' Isolde ein:

That deep, inscrutable,
mysterious hidden cause—
who'll make it manifest?

ᴛʀɪsᴛᴀɴ *(raising his eyes sympathizingly to Mark)*:
O Sov'reign, I
cannot truly tell you;
and what you ask
can never have an answer.
(He turns toward Isolde, who looks up long-
ingly to him.)
Now whither Tristan travels,
will you, Isolde, follow?
The land that Tristan means
no sunlight can illume:
it is the dark
nocturnal land
from whence my mother
sent me forth
when, in the throes of
death they bore me;
in dying
she gave me to daylight's kingdom.
From the time I was born
her loving refuge was
the wonder-realm of night,
from where I woke to light.
Such Tristan offers you,
and first he goes before;
if she will follow,
kind and true,
let Isold' speak right now!

ɪsᴏʟᴅᴇ:
Once, when a friend did
woo her for a foreign land,
the one kind and
gracious followed
the unkind master.
Now lead to your dominions,
your heritage to show me;
how should I flee that land
that spans the wide world round?
Where Tristan has his home
there will Isolde stay:

auf dem sie folge
treu und hold,
den Weg nun zeig Isold'!
(*Tristan neigt sich langsam über sie und
küßt sie sanft auf die Stirn. — Melot fährt
wütend auf.*)

MELOT (*das Schwert ziehend*):
Verräter! Ha!
Zur Rache, König!
Duldest du diese Schmach?
(*Tristan zieht sein Schwert und wendet sich
schnell um.*)

TRISTAN:
Wer wagt sein Leben an das meine?
(*Er heftet den Blick auf Melot.*)
Mein Freund war der,
er minnte mich hoch und teuer;
um Ehr' und Ruhm
nir war er besorgt wie keiner.
Zum Übermut
trieb er mein Herz;
die Schar führt' er,
die mich gedrängt,
Ehr' und Ruhm mir zu mehren,
dem König dich zu vermählen!
Dein Blick, Isolde,
blendet' auch ihn;
aus Eifer verriet
mich der Freund
dem König, den ich verriet!
(*Er dringt auf Melot ein.*)
Wehr dich, Melot!
(*Als Melot ihm das Schwert entgegenstreckt,
läßt Tristan das seinige fallen und sinkt verwundet in Kurwenals Arme. Isolde stürzt
sich an seine Brust. Marke hält Melot
zurück. Der Vorhang fällt schnell.*)

the way she follows,
kind and true,
that way now show Isold'!

*Tristan bends slowly down to her and kisses
her gently on her forehead. Melot starts
angrily forward.*

MELOT *(drawing his sword):*
You traitor! Ha!
My king, take vengeance!
Will you bear such a shame?

TRISTAN *(draws his sword and turns quickly round):*
Who dares to pit his life against mine?
(Fixing his gaze on Melot.)
My friend was he,
he loved me dearly and truly;
none cared so much
about my fame and my honor.
He made my heart
arrogant-proud;
he led forces
that urged me act,
make an increase to honor,
by wedding you to our monarch!
Your glance, Isolde,
dazzled him, too,
and passion then made
him betray
to the monarch, whom I betrayed!
(He sets on Melot.)
On guard, Melot!

*As Melot thrusts his sword at him, Tristan
lets his fall and sinks wounded into Kurvenal's arms; Isolde throws herself upon his
breast. Mark holds back Melot. The curtain
falls quickly.*

CURTAIN

DRITTER AUFZUG

Burggarten zur einen Seite hohe Burggebäude, zur andren eine niedrige Mauerbrüstung, von einer Warte unterbrochen; im Hintergrunde das Burgtor. Die Lage ist auf felsiger Höhe anzunehmen; durch Öffnungen blickt man auf einen weiten Meereshorizont. Das Ganze macht den Eindruck der Herrenlosigkeit, übel, gepflegt, hie und da schadhaft und bewachsen. Im Vordergrunde, an der inneren Seite, liegt Tristan, unter dem Schatten einer großen Linde, auf einem Ruhebett schlafend, wie leblos ausgestreckt. Zu Häupten ihm sitzt Kurwenal, in Schmerz über ihn hingebeugt und sorgsam seinem Atem lauschend. Von der Außenseite her hört man, beim Aufziehen des Vorhanges, einen Hirtenreigen, sehnsüchtig und traurig auf einer Schalmei geblasen. Endlich erscheint der Hirt selbst mit dem Oberleibe über der Mauerbrüstung und blickt teilnehmend herein.

ERSTER AUFTRITT

Der Hirt. Kurwenal. Tristan.

HIRT *(leise)*: Kurwenal! He!
Sag, Kurwenal!
Hör doch, Freund!
(Kurwenal wendet ein wenig das Haupt nach ihm.)

KURWENAL *(schüttelt traurig mit dem Kopf)*:
Erwachte er,
wär's doch nur,
um für immer zu verscheiden:
erschien zuvor
die Ärztin nicht,
die einz'ge, die uns hilft. —
Sahst du noch nichts?
Kein Schiff noch auf der See?

ACT III

SCENE I

The garden of a castle. At one side are high turrets; on the other is a low breastwork broken by a watchtower; at back, the castle gate. The site is on rocky cliffs; through openings one looks over a wide sea to the horizon. The whole scene gives an impression of being ownerless, badly kept, here and there dilapidated and overgrown.

In the foreground inside lies Tristan sleeping on a couch, under the shade of a great lime tree. He is extended as if lifeless. At his head sits Kurvenal, bending over him in grief, and anxiously listening to his breathing. From without comes the sound of a shepherd's pipe. The upper half of the shepherd's body shows over the breastwork as he looks on sympathetically.

SHEPHERD: Kurvenal! Hey!

           Kurvenal turns his head a little toward him.

           Say, Kurvenal!
           Hear me, friend!
           Has he not waked?

KURVENAL *(shaking his head sadly)*:
           Were he to wake,
           it would be
           just to part from us forever:
           unless there comes
           the one who heals,
           for she alone can help.
           What have you seen?
           No ship yet on the sea?

HIRT: Eine andre Weise
                         hörtest du dann,
                         so lustig, als ich sie nur kann.
                         Nun sag auch ehrlich,
                         alter Freund:
                         was hat's mit unserm Herrn?

KURWENAL: Laß die Frage:
                         du kannst's doch nie erfahren.
                         Eifrig späh,
                         und siehst du ein Schiff,
                         so spiele lustig und hell!
                         *(Der Hirt wendet sich und späht, mit der
                         Hand überm Auge, nach dem Meer aus.)*

HIRT: Öd und leer das Meer!
                         *(Er setzt die Schalmei an den Mund und
                         entfernt sich blasend.)*

TRISTAN *(bewegungslos, dumpf)*:
                         Die alte Weise; —
                         Was weckt sie mich?

KURWENAL *(fährt erschrocken auf)*:
                         Ha!

TRISTAN *(schlägt die Augen auf und wendet das Haupt ein
     wenig)*:
                         Wo bin ich?

KURWENAL: Ha! Diese Stimme!
                         Seine Stimme!
                         Tristan! Herre!
                         Mein Held! Mein Tristan!

TRISTAN *(mit Anstrengung)*:
                         Wer ruft mich?

KURWENAL: Endlich! Endlich!
                         Leben, o Leben!
                         Süßes Leben,
                         meinem Tristan neu gegeben!

TRISTAN *(ein wenig auf dem Lager sich erhebend, matt)*:
                         Kurwenal — du?
                         Wo war ich?
                         Wo bin ich?

SHEPHERD: I would play you quite a
different tune,
as merry a one as I could.
Now tell me rightly,
trusty friend:
how goes it with our lord?

KURVENAL: Leave that question:
you cannot learn by asking.
Scan the sea,
and if you see sails,
then pipe out blithely and clear!

*The shepherd turns round and scans the sea,
shading his eyes with his hand.*

SHEPHERD: Bleak and bare the sea!
*(He puts the pipe to his mouth and with-
draws, playing.)*

TRISTAN *(without moving, faintly)*:
Why does it wake me—
that ancient tune?
*(He opens his eyes and turns his head a
little.)*

KURVENAL *(with a start of surprise)*:
Ha!

TRISTAN: Where am I?

KURVENAL: Now I hear him!
He is speaking!
Tristan! Master!
My lord! My hero!

TRISTAN *(with effort)*:
Who calls me?

KURVENAL: Life! At last comes
life for my hero!
Life, sweet life, given
anew to bless my Tristan!

TRISTAN *(feebly)*:
Kurvenal, you?
Where was I?
Where am I?

KURWENAL: Wo du bist?
In Frieden, sicher und frei!
Kareol, Herr:
kennst du die Burg
der Väter nicht?

TRISTAN: Meiner Väter?

KURWENAL: Sieh dich nur um!

TRISTAN: Was erklang mir?

KURWENAL: Des Hirten Weise
hörtest du wieder;
am Hügel ab
hütet er deine Herde.

TRISTAN: Meine Herde?

KURWENAL: Herr, das mein' ich!
Dein das Haus,
Hof und Burg!
Das Volk, getreu
dem trauten Herrn,
so gut es konnt',
hat's Haus und Hof gepflegt,
das einst mein Held
zu Erb' und Eigen
an Leut' und Volk verschenkt,
als alles er verließ,
in fremde Land' zu ziehn.

TRISTAN: In welches Land?

KURWENAL: Hei! Nach Kornwall:
kühn und wonnig,
was sich da Glanzes,
Glückes und Ehren
Tristan, mein Held, hehr ertrotzt!

TRISTAN: Bin ich in Kornwall?

KURWENAL: Nicht doch: in Kareol!

TRISTAN: Wie kam ich her?

KURWENAL: Hei nun! Wie du kamst?
Zu Roß rittest du nicht;

KURVENAL:	Where are you? In peace that's free and secure! Kareol, lord: do you not know your father's halls?
TRISTAN:	How? My father's?
KURVENAL:	Just look around!
TRISTAN:	What just sounded?
KURVENAL:	Again you heard the shepherd's tune sounding; He tends your flocks over there on the hillside.
TRISTAN:	Are they my flocks?
KURVENAL:	Sire, I say so! Yours are house, court, and fort! The folk who truly love their lord as best they could have kept the house and court that once my hero did bequeath to his vassals and his serfs, that time he left all here to hie to foreign land.
TRISTAN:	What foreign land?
KURVENAL:	Why, to Cornwall: where my Tristan, brave and gallant, proudly defiant, won fortune, honors, and fame!
TRISTAN:	Am I in Cornwall?
KURVENAL:	Not now: in Kareol.
TRISTAN:	How came I here?
KURVENAL:	Well, now! How you came? You rode not on a horse;

ein Schifflein führte dich her.
Doch zu dem Schifflein
hier auf den Schultern
trug ich dich; — die sind breit:
sie trugen dich dort zum Strand.
Nun bist du daheim, daheim zu Land:
im echten Land,
im Heimatland;
auf eigner Weid' und Wonne,
im Schein der alten Sonne,
darin von Tod und Wunden
du selig sollst gesunden.
(Er schmiegt sich an Tristans Brust.)

TRISTAN *(nach einem kleinen Schweigen):*
Dünkt dich das?
Ich weiß es anders,
doch kann ich's dir nicht sagen.
Wo ich erwacht —
weilt' ich nicht;
doch, wo ich weilte,
das kann ich dir nicht sagen.
Die Sonne sah ich nicht,
noch sah ich Land und Leute:
doch, was ich sah,
das kann ich dir nicht sagen.
Ich war,
wo ich von je gewesen,
wohin auf je ich geh':
im weiten Reich
der Weltennacht.
Nur ein Wissen
dort uns eigen:
göttlich ew'ges
Ur-Vergessen!
Wie schwand mir seine Ahnung?
Sehnsücht'ge Mahnung,
nenn' ich dich,
die neu dem Licht
des Tags mich zugetrieben?
Was einzig mir geblieben;
ein heiß-inbrünstig Lieben,
aus Todes-Wonne-Grauen

a small ship carried you here:
I bore you on my
shoulders and brought you
to the boat;
they are broad:
they carried you to the shore.
Now you are at home, at home on land,
in your own land,
your native land;
among your happy pastures,
the old sun's rays will heal you;
from death and all your wounds you
shall blessedly recover.
(He clings to Tristan's breast.)

TRISTAN: Think you so?
I know it better,
and yet I cannot tell it.
I did not stay—
where I woke;
yet where I tarried,
I cannot really tell you.
The sun I did not see,
nor saw I land and people:
yet, what I saw,
I can indeed not tell you.
I was
where I have been forever,
where I forever go:
the realm of night
which girds the world.
We have there one knowledge only:
godlike, endless
prime oblivion!
How did foreknowledge vanish?
Yearning monition,
is it such,
that drives me back
into the realm of daylight?
All that survived within me,
a love ardent and burning,
that drives me forth from death's dread

jagt's mich, das Licht zu schauen,
das trügend hell und golden
noch dir, Isolden, scheint!
(Kurwenal birgt, von Grausen gepackt, sein
Haupt. Tristan richtet sich allmählich immer
mehr auf.)
Isolde noch
im Reich der Sonne!
Im Tagesschimmer
noch Isolde!
Welches Sehnen!
Welches Bangen!
Sie zu sehen,
welch Verlangen!
Krachend hört' ich
hinter mir
schon des Todes
Tor sich schließen:
weit nun steht es
wieder offen,
der Sonne Strahlen
sprengt' es auf;
mit hell erschloßnen Augen
mußt' ich der Nacht enttauchen —
sie zu suchen,
sie zu sehen;
sie zu finden,
in der einzig
zu vergehen,
zu entschwinden
Tristan ist vergönnt.
Weh, nun wächst,
bleich und bang,
mir des Tages
wilder Drang;
grell und täuschend
sein Gestirn
weckt zu Trug
und Wahn mir das Hirn!
Verfluchter Tag
mit deinem Schein!
Wachst du ewig
meiner Pein?

rapture to look on daylight,
that falsely bright and golden,
still on you, Isolde, shines!
Isolde still in realms of sunlight!
The land of day still holds Isolde!
Ah, what longing!
What dread fretting!
What a yearning
now to see her!
Crashing sounds I've
heard already
when death's door
slammed behind me:
now again that
door stands open;
the streaming sunlight
burst it wide:
with clear, wide-open eyes I
must rise from out night's kingdom,
just to seek her,
just to see her,
just to find the
one in whom
alone I'll lose myself,
in whom alone
I cease to be.
Woe, now comes,
pale and fearful,
the wild distress of day;
dazzling speciously,
its eye
wakes my brain
to fraud and delusion!
Accursed day,
accursed glare!
Must you ever
wake my woe?

> Brennt sie ewig,
> diese Leuchte,
> die selbst nachts
> von ihr mich scheuchte?
> Ach, Isolde,
> süße Holde!
> Wann endlich,
> wann, ach wann
> löschest du die Zünde,
> daß sie mein Glück mir künde?
> Das Licht — wann löscht es aus?
> *(Er sinkt erschöpft leise zurück.)*
> Wann wird es Nacht im Haus?

KURWENAL *(nach großer Erschütterung aus der Nieder-*
geschlagenheit sich aufraffend):

> Der einst ich trotzt',
> aus Treu' zu dir,
> mit dir nach ihr
> nun muß ich mich sehnen.
> Glaub meinem Wort:
> du sollst sie sehen
> hier und heut;
> den Trost kann ich dir geben —
> ist sie nur selbst noch am Leben.

TRISTAN *(sehr matt):*

> Noch losch das Licht nicht aus,
> noch ward's nicht Nacht im Haus:
> Isolde lebt und wacht;
> sie rief mich aus der Nacht.

KURWENAL:

> Lebt sie denn,
> so laß dir Hoffnung lachen!
> Muß Kurwenal dumm dir gelten,
> heut sollst du ihn nicht schelten.
> Wie tot lagst du
> seit dem Tag,
> da Melot, der Verruchte,
> dir eine Wunde schlug.
> Die böse Wunde,
> wie sie heilen?
> Mir tör'gem Manne
> dünkt' es da,

        Must that beacon
burn forever,
making nights
a fear to see her?
Ah, Isolde,
sweet and gracious!
When, finally,
will you
quench the beacon signal,
that it announce my happiness?
The light, when will it die?
(He sinks back gently, exhausted.)
When will the house be still?

KURVENAL: Whom once I braved,
through faith in you,
I now do long
for, just the way you do.
Trust in my word:
I know you'll see her,
here, today:
that solace I can give you,
if only she still be living.

TRISTAN *(very faintly)*:
        The light is not yet out,
the house is still not dark:
Isolde lives and wakes;
she called me from the night.

KURVENAL: If she lives,
then let this hope console you!
Though Kurvenal seem quite simple,
today you shall not blame him.
As dead I have
seen you lie
since Melot, the accursed,
dealt you a heavy wound.
This wound so grievous—
how to heal it?
I, foolish fellow,
had the thought

wer einst dir Morolds
Wunde schloß,
der heilte leicht die Plagen
von Melots Wehr geschlagen.
Die beste Ärztin
bald ich fand;
nach Kornwall hab' ich
ausgesandt:
ein treuer Mann
wohl übers Meer
bringt dir Isolden her.

TRISTAN (außer sich):
Isolde kommt!
Isolde naht!
(Er ringt gleichsam nach Sprache.)
O Treue! Hehre,
holde Treue!
(Er zieht Kurwenal an sich und umarmt ihn.)
Mein Kurwenal,
du trauter Freund!
Du Treuer ohne Wanken,
wie soll dir Tristan danken?
Mein Schild, mein Schirm
in Kampf und Streit,
zu Lust und Leid
mir stets bereit:
wen ich gehaßt,
den haßtest du;
wen ich geminnt,
den minntest du.
Dem guten Marke,
dient' ich ihm hold,
wie warst du ihm treuer als Gold!
Mußt' ich verraten
den edlen Herrn,
wie betrogst du ihn da so gern!
Dir nicht eigen,
einzig mein,
mit leidest du,
wenn ich leide:
nur was ich leide,
das kannst du nicht leiden!

that she, who once healed
Morold's wounds,
could quickly heal the injury
that Melot's weapon dealt you.
I found the best
physician soon;
I've summoned her from
Cornwall's shores:
a trusty man
soon will arrive,
bringing Isolde here.

TRISTAN *(transported)*:

Isolde comes!
Isold' draws nigh!
(He struggles to find words.)
O constancy!
Lofty, lovely loyalty!
(He draws Kurvenal toward him and embraces him.)
O Kurvenal,
my trusty friend!
Most loyal, never wav'ring,
how shall your Tristan thank you?
My shield, my fort
in war and strife,
one always there
through weal or woe:
whom I did hate,
you hated, too;
whom I have loved,
you loved, as well.
When truly serving
kindly King Mark,
you were to him truer than gold!
When I betrayed, though,
my noble lord,
how you gladly betrayed him too!
Yours you are not,
only mine;
you suffer too,
when I suffer;
that can you not suffer!

Dies furchtbare Schnen,
das mich sehrt;
dies schmachtende Brennen,
das mich zehrt;
wollt' ich dir's nennen,
könntest du's kennen:
nicht hier würdest du weilen,
zur Warte müßtest du eilen —
mit allen Sinnen
sehnend von hinnen
nach dorten trachten und spähen,
wo ihre Segel sich blähen,
wo vor den Winden,
mich zu finden,
von der Liebe Drang befeuert,
Isolde zu mir steuert! —
Es naht! Es naht
mit mutiger Hast!
Sie weht, sie weht —
die Flagge am Mast.
Das Schiff! Das Schiff!
Dort streicht es am Riff!
Siehst du es nicht? *(Heftig.)*
Kurwenal, siehst du es nicht?
*(Als Kurwenal, um Tristan nicht zu ver-
lassen, zögert, und dieser in schweigender
Spannung auf ihn blickt, ertönt, wie zu
Anfang, näher, dann ferner, die klagende
Weise des Hirten.)*

KURWENAL *(niedergeschlagen)*:
Noch ist kein Schiff zu sehn!

TRISTAN *(hat mit abnehmender Aufregung gelauscht und
beginnt nun mit wachsender Schwermut)*:
Muß ich dich so verstehn,
du alte ernste Weise,
mit deiner Klage Klang?
Durch Abendwehen
drang sie bang,
als einst dem Kind
des Vaters Tod verkündet.
Durch Morgengrauen
bang und bänger,

This terrible yearning
sears my soul;
this languishing burning
that consumes;
if I would tell it,
if you could know it:
no more here would you tarry,
you'd have to haste to the tower,
with all your senses
longingly straining
and seaward striving and watching,
where now her sails must be spreading,
and winds assisting,
where to find me;
fired by driving love's impatience,
Isold' is steering to me.
She comes, she comes,
with valorous haste!
It waves, it waves,
the flag on the masthead!
The ship! The ship!
It cleaves through the reef!
Do you not see?
Kurvenal! Do you not see?

*As Kurvenal hesitates to leave Tristan, who
gazes at him in mute expectation, the mourn-
ful tune of the shepherd is heard, as at the
beginning.*

KURVENAL *(dejectedly)*:
Still there's no ship to see.

*Tristan has listened with waning excitement,
and now begins to speak with growing melancholy.*

TRISTAN:
Must I explain you thus,
you air so old and solemn,
with your so plaintive sound?
Through evening air your
sound was dread,
when once a child
was piped his father's passing;
through morning grayness,
still more fearful,

als der Sohn
der Mutter Los vernahm.
Da er mich zeugt' und starb,
sie sterbend mich gebar.
Die alte Weise
sehnsuchtbang
zu ihnen wohl
auch klagend drang,
die einst mich frug
und jetzt mich frägt:
zu welchem Los erkoren,
ich damals wohl geboren?
Zu welchem Los?
Die alte Weise
sagt mir's wieder:
mich sehnen — und sterben!
Nein! Ach nein!
So heißt sie nicht!
Sehnen! Sehnen!
Im Sterben mich zu sehnen,
vor Sehnsucht nicht zu sterben!
Die nie erstirbt,
sehnend nun ruft
um Sterbens Ruh
sie der fernen Ärztin zu. —
Sterbend lag ich
stumm im Kahn,
der Wunde Gift
dem Herzen nah:
Sehnsucht klagend
klang die Weise;
den Segel blähte der Wind
hin zu Irlands Kind.
Die Wunde, die
sie heilend schloß,
riß mit dem Schwert
sie wieder los;
das Schwert dann aber —
ließ sie sinken;
den Gifttrank gab sie
mir zu trinken:
wie ich da hoffte
ganz zu genesen,

when the son
was told his mother's fate.
He died before my birth,
when I was born, she died;
the ancient song of
boding longing
gave wailing sounds
they must have heard;
it asked me once,
and asks me now:
What fate was I allotted,
the day my mother bore me?
What is my fate?
That strain so ancient
once more tells me:
of yearning and dying!
No! Ah, no!
It bids not that!
Yearning! Yearning!
In dying I must yearn on,
but must not die of yearning.
What never dies,
yearningly calls
the distant healer
and asks for death's repose.
Dying, I lay
mute on deck,
the poisoned wound
was near my heart:
drear the song, and
melancholy;
the breezes filling the sails
urged to Ireland's child.
The wound her healing
hand had closed
she opened once
more with her sword,
the sword then—after—
she relinquished;
the poisoned potion
that she gave me,
I hoped it would
completely restore me;

da ward der sehrendste
Zauber erlesen:
daß nie ich sollte sterben,
mich ew'ger Qual vererben!
Der Trank! Der Trank!
Der furchtbare Trank!
Wie vom Herz zum Hirn
er wütend mir drang!
Kein Heil nun kann,
kein süßer Tod
je mich befrein
von der Sehnsucht Not;
nirgends, ach nirgends
find' ich Ruh:
mich wirft die Nacht
dem Tage zu,
um ewig an meinen Leiden
der Sonne Auge zu weiden.
O dieser Sonne
sengender Strahl,
wie brennt mir das Hirn
seine glühende Qual!
Für dieser Hitze
heißes Verschmachten,
ach, keines Schattens
kühlend Umnachten!
Für dieser Schmerzen
schreckliche Pein,
welcher Balsam sollte
mir Lindrung verleihn?
Den furchtbaren Trank,
der der Qual mich vertraut,
ich selbst — ich selbst,
ich hab' ihn gebraut!
Aus Vaters Not
und Mutterweh,
aus Liebestränen
eh und je —
aus Lachen und Weinen,
Wonnen und Wunden
hab' ich des Trankes
Gifte gefunden!
Den ich gebraut,

its searing magic, though,
had for intention
that death should never find me,
but endless torment take me!
The drink!
The drink, the terrible drink!
How from heart to head
it filled me with fire!
No healing art,
nor kindly death
can make me free
from this yearning need.
Nowhere, ah, nowhere
find I rest;
I'm cast by night
into the day,
where sun's gloating eye is ever
the witness to all my sorrow.
Oh, how the scorching
glare of the sun
does blister my brain
with its torturing glow!
Against this heat that
withers and parches,
there comes no help from
night's cooling darkness.
Against this great and
terrible pain,
where's balsam that can
bring healing relief?
The horrible drink
with the torment it gave—
myself, myself
caused it to be brewed!
My father's grief
and mother's woe,
the tears of love
to come, and past,
the laughing and weeping,
joying and wounding—
these did I make a
poisonous potion.
What was then brewed,

der mir geflossen,
den wonneschlürfend
je ich genossen —
verflucht sei, furchtbarer Trank!
Verflucht, wer dich gebraut!
(*Er sinkt ohnmächtig zurück.*)

KURWENAL (*der vergebens Tristan zu mäßigen suchte, schreit
entsetzt auf*):

Mein Herre! Tristan!
Schrecklicher Zauber!
O Minnetrug!
O Liebeszwang!
Der Welt holdester Wahn,
wie ist's um dich getan!
Hier liegt er nun,
der wonnige Mann,
der wie keiner geliebt und geminnt.
Nun seht, was von ihm
sie Dankes gewann,
was je Minne sich gewinnt!
(*Mit schluchzender Stimme.*)
Bist du nun tot?
Lebst du noch?
Hat dich der Fluch entführt?
(*Er lauscht seinem Atem.*)
O Wonne! Nein!
Er regt sich, er lebt!
Wie sanft er die Lippen rührt!

TRISTAN (*langsam wieder zu sich kommend*):

Das Schiff? Siehst du's noch nicht?

KURWENAL:

Das Schiff? Gewiß,
es naht noch heut;
es kann nicht lang mehr säumen.

TRISTAN:

Und drauf Isolde,
wie sie winkt —
wie sie hold
mir Sühne trinkt.
Siehst du sie?
Siehst du sie noch nicht?
Wie sie selig,

what I had taken,
that ever gave me
joy in the sipping.
I curse you, terrible drink!
Accursed who made your brew!

KURVENAL *(who has been vainly striving to calm Tristan, cries out in terror)*:
Frightful enchantment!
Oh, love's deceit!
Oh, passion's pow'r!
The world's loveliest dream!
What is this you have done!
here lies he now,
the rarest of men,
no one like him so loved and adored!
Behold, what return
his love has obtained,
which is all love ever wins.
(His voice broken by sobs.)
Are you now dead?
Do you live?
Have you fulfilled the curse?
(He listens for his breath.)
O rapture! No!
He's stirring! He lives!
How gently he moves his lips!

TRISTAN *(beginning very faintly)*:
The ship? Is it in sight?

KURVENAL:
The ship? Indeed,
it comes today:
it can't delay much longer.

TRISTAN:
On board, Isolde,
how she waves,
how she sweetly
drinks our peace:
Do you see?
Can't you see her yet?
How she, blest and

hehr und milde
wandelt durch
des Meers Gefilde?
Auf wonniger Blumen
lichten Wogen
kommt sie sanft
ans Land gezogen.
Sie lächelt mir Trost
und süße Ruh,
sie führt mir letzte
Labung zu.
Ach, Isolde! Isolde!
Wie schön bist du!
Und Kurwenal, wie,
du sähst sie nicht?
Hinauf zur Warte,
du blöder Wicht!
Was so hell und licht ich sehe,
daß das dir nicht entgehe!
Hörst du mich nicht?
Zur Warte schnell!
Eilig zur Warte!
Bist du zur Stell'?
Das Schiff? Das Schiff?
Isoldens Schiff?
Du mußt es sehen!
Mußt es sehen!
Das Schiff? Sähst du's noch nicht?
(Während Kurwenal noch zögernd mit Tris-
tan ringt, läßt der Hirt von außen die Schal-
mei ertönen. Kurwenal springt freudig auf.)

KURWENAL: O Wonne! Freude!
                 (Er stürzt auf die Warte und späht aus.)
                 Ha! Das Schiff!
                 Von Norden seh' ich's nahen.

TRISTAN *(in wachsender Begeisterung):*
                 Wußt' ich's nicht?
                 Sagt' ich's nicht,
                 daß sie noch lebt,
                 noch Leben mir webt?
                 Die mir Isolde

mild and noble,
makes her way
through sea's expanses?
On luminous waves of
lovely flowers,
see her draw
to gentle landing.
Her smile brings me peace
and sweet repose,
she gives me
uttermost relief.
Ah, Isolde! Isolde!
How fair you are!
And Kurvenal, how,
you saw her not?
Go up the watchtow'r,
you purblind wretch!
What I saw so bright and clearly
make sure it not escapes you.
Do you not hear?
The watchtow'r, quick!
Haste to the watchtow'r!
Are you still here?
The ship? The ship?
Isolde's ship!
You have to see it!
You must see it!
The ship? Don't you see it?

*Whilst Kurvenal, still hesitating, opposes
Tristan, the shepherd's merry piping is heard
without.*

KURVENAL: O rapture!
                Marv'lous!
                (He rushes to the watchtower and looks out.)
                Ha! The ship!
                From northward it is coming.

TRISTAN: Did I know?
                Was I right?
                That she still lives,
                still knits me to life.
                For me the world
                contains only Isolde,

einzig enthält,
wie wär' Isolde
mir aus der Welt?

KURWENAL *(von der Warte zurückrufend, jauchzend)*:
Heiha! Heiha!
Wie es mutig steuert!
Wie stark der Segel sich bläht!
Wie es jagt, wie es fliegt!

TRISTAN: Die Flagge? Die Flagge?

KURWENAL: Der Freude Flagge
am Wimpel lustig und hell!

TRISTAN *(auf dem Lager hoch sich aufrichtend)*:
Hahei! Der Freude!
Hell am Tage
zu mir Isolde!
Isolde zu mir!
Siehst du sie selbst?

KURWENAL: Jetzt schwand das Schiff
hinter dem Fels.

TRISTAN: Hinter dem Riff?
Bringt es Gefahr?
Dort wütet die Brandung,
scheitern die Schiffe!
Das Steuer, wer führt's?

KURWENAL: Der sicherste Seemann.

TRISTAN: Verriet' er mich?
Wär' er Melots Genoß?

KURWENAL: Trau ihm wie mir!

TRISTAN: Verräter auch du!
Unsel'ger!
Siehst du sie wieder?

KURWENAL: Noch nicht.

TRISTAN: Verloren!

how then could
she leave the world!

KURVENAL *(shouting)*:
Ahoy! Ahoy!
See it bravely tacking!
The sail is full with the wind!
How it drives, how it plies!

TRISTAN: The pennant! The pennant!

KURVENAL: The joyful pennant
at topmast, merry and bright!

TRISTAN *(raising himself up from his couch)*:
Ahoy, what rapture!
Bright the day
that has brought Isolde!
Isolde comes here!
D'you see her there?

KURVENAL: It went, just now,
hid by the rock.

TRISTAN: Hid by the reef?
Is there some risk?
There breakers are raging,
vessels have foundered!
Who stands at the helm?

KURVENAL: The surest of seamen.

TRISTAN: Has he betrayed?
Could he be Melot's friend?

KURVENAL: Trust him like me!

TRISTAN: A traitor like you!
Unblest one!
Has it come back yet?

KURVENAL: Not yet.

TRISTAN: It's done for!

KURWENAL *(jauchzend)*:
>   Heiha! Hei ha ha ha ha!
>   Vorbei! Vorbei!
>   Glücklich vorbei!

TRISTAN *(jauchzend)*:
>   Kurwenal, hei ha ha ha!
>   treuester Freund!
>   All mein Hab und Gut
>   vererb' ich noch heute.

KURWENAL: Sie nahen im Flug.

TRISTAN: Siehst du sie endlich?
>   Siehst du Isolde?

KURWENAL: Sie ist's! Sie winkt!

TRISTAN: O seligstes Weib!

KURWENAL: Im Hafen der Kiel!
>   Isolde, ha!
>   Mit einem Sprung
>   springt sie vom Bord ans **Land.**

TRISTAN: Herab von der Warte,
>   müßiger Gaffer!
>   Hinab! Hinab
>   an den Strand!
>   Hilf ihr! Hilf meiner Frau!

KURWENAL: Sie trag' ich herauf:
>   trau meinen Armen!
>   Doch du, Tristan,
>   bleib mir treulich am Bett.
>   *(Kurwenal eilt fort.)*

KURVENAL (*shouting*):

Ahoy, ahoy, ahoy!
They're past, they're through,
safely, they're through!

TRISTAN:

Ahoy, ahoy! Kurvenal,
truest of friends!
All my worldly goods
today I bequeath you.

KURVENAL:

They're coming full speed!

TRISTAN:

Now can you see her?

KURVENAL:

It's she! She waves!

TRISTAN:

O woman most blest!

KURVENAL:

The vessel is home!
Isolde, ha!
a single spring
brings her from deck to land.

TRISTAN:

Get down from the watchtow'r,
indolent gaper!
Get down! Get down
to the shore!
Help her! Help my beloved!

KURVENAL:

I'll bring her up here:
trust I can do it!
But you, Tristan,
stay right there on your couch.
(*Kurvenal hastens away.*)

Zweiter Auftritt

Tristan. Isolde. Kurwenal.

TRISTAN (*in höchster Aufregung auf dem Lager sich mühend*):
　　　　　O diese Sonne!
　　　　　Ha, dieser Tag!
　　　　　Ha, dieser Wonne
　　　　　sonnigster Tag!
　　　　　Jagendes Blut,
　　　　　jauchzender Mut!
　　　　　Lust ohne Maßen,
　　　　　freudiges Rasen!
　　　　　Auf des Lagers Bann
　　　　　wie sie ertragen!
　　　　　Wohlauf und daran,
　　　　　wo die Herzen schlagen!
　　　　　Tristan der Held,
　　　　　in jubelnder Kraft,
　　　　　hat sich vom Tod
　　　　　emporgerafft!
　　　　　(*Er richtet sich hoch auf.*)
　　　　　Mit blutender Wunde
　　　　　bekämpft' ich einst Morolden,
　　　　　mit blutender Wunde
　　　　　erjag' ich mir heut Isolden!
　　　　　(*Er reißt sich den Verband der Wunde auf.*)
　　　　　Heia, mein Blut!
　　　　　Lustig nun fließe!
　　　　　(*Er springt vom Lager herab und schwankt
　　　　　vorwärts.*)
　　　　　Die mir die Wunde
　　　　　auf ewig schließe —
　　　　　sie naht wie ein Held,
　　　　　sie naht mir zum Heil!
　　　　　Vergeh' die Welt
　　　　　meiner jauchzenden Eil'!
　　　　　(*Er taumelt nach der Mitte der Bühne.*)

ISOLDE (*von außen*):
　　　　　Tristan! Geliebter!

SCENE II

TRISTAN *(tossing on his couch in extreme excitement)*:
   O blessed sunlight!
   Ha, what a day!
   Ha, what a joyful,
   radiant day!
   Tumult of blood,
   jubilant pow'r!
   Measureless pleasure!
   Joyful delirium!
   When confined to bed
   how can I bear them?
   Well, up then and off
   to where hearts are beating!
   Tristan, the knight,
   in jubilant strength,
   has dragged himself
   away from death!
   (He raises himself quite up.)
   My wound was all bleeding
   when once I fought with Morold:
   so, bleeding it shall be
   in struggling to have Isolde!
   (He tears the bandage from his wound.)
   Aha, my blood!
   flow now, exulting!
   (He springs from his bed and staggers for-
   ward.)
   She who can close my
   wound forever
   most valiantly comes,
   she comes for my good!
   let earth now pass
   in my jubilant haste!
   (He totters to the center of the stage.)

ISOLDE *(without)*: Tristan! Beloved!

TRISTAN *(in der furchtbarsten Aufregung)*:
Wie, hör' ich das Licht?
Die Leuchte, ha!
Die Leuchte verlischt!
Zu ihr! Zu ihr!
(Isolde eilt atemlos herein. Tristan, seiner nicht mächtig, stürzt sich ihr schwankend entgegen. In der Mitte der Bühne begegnen sie sich; sie empfängt ihn in ihren Armen. Tristan sinkt langsam in ihren Armen zu Boden.)

ISOLDE: Tristan! Ha!

TRISTAN *(sterbend zu ihr aufblickend)*:
Isolde! *(Er stirbt.)*

ISOLDE: Ha! Ich bin's, ich bin's,
süßester Freund!
Auf, noch einmal
hör meinen Ruf!
Isolde ruft:
Isolde kam,
mit Tristan treu zu sterben.
Bleibst du mir stumm?
Nur eine Stunde,
nur eine Stunde
bleibe mir wach!
So bange Tage
wachte sie sehnend,
um eine Stunde
mit dir noch zu wachen:
betrügt Isolden,
betrügt sie Tristan
um dieses einzige,
ewig kurze
letzte Weltenglück?
Die Wunde? Wo?
Laß sie mich heilen!
Daß wonnig und hehr
die Nacht wir teilen;
nicht an der Wunde,
an der Wunde stirb mir nicht:

TRISTAN *(in frantic excitement):*
> Can I hear the light?
> The torchlight, ha!
> The torchlight is quenched!
> To her! To her!

> *Isolde hastens breathlessly in. Tristan, out of his senses, staggers weakly toward her. They meet in the center of the stage; she receives him in her arms.*

ISOLDE *(as Tristan sinks slowly to the ground in Isolde's arms):*
> Tristan! Ha!

TRISTAN *(raising his eyes to Isolde):*
> Isolde!
> *(He dies.)*

ISOLDE:
> Ha!
> It's I, it's I,
> sweetest of friends!
> Up, this once more
> hear when I call!
> Isolde calls:
> Isolde's here
> to loy'lly die with Tristan!
> Will you not speak?
> Only an hour,
> only an hour
> stay awake, love!
> I've spent such days in
> anxiously yearning,
> that I might wake with
> you for one short hour.
> Will you deceive me,
> deceive Isolde
> of even this single,
> swiftly fleeting,
> final earthly joy?
> The wound is where?
> Oh, let me heal it,
> that, raptured, we share
> the night together!
> Oh, do not perish
> of your wound, oh. do not die:

uns beiden vereint
erlösche das Lebenslicht!
Gebrochen der Blick!
Still das Herz!
Nicht eines Atems
flücht'ges Wehn! —
Muß sie nun jammernd
vor dir stehn,
die sich wonnig dir zu vermählen
mutig kam übers Meer?
Zu spät!
Trotziger Mann!
Strafst du mich so
mit härtestem Bann?
Ganz ohne Huld
meiner Leidens-Schuld?
Nicht meine Klagen
darf ich dir sagen?
Nur einmal, ach!
nur einmal noch! —
Tristan! — Ha! —
Horch! Er wacht!
Geliebter!
(Sie sinkt bewußtlos über der Leiche zusammen.)

(Kurwenal war sogleich hinter Isolde zurückgekommen; sprachlos in furchtbarer Erschütterung hat er dem Auftritte beigewohnt und bewegungslos auf Tristan hingestarrt. Aus der Tiefe hört man jetzt dumpfes Gemurmel und Waffengeklirr. Der Hirt kommt über die Mauer gestiegen.)

let us both together
made one, lose the light of life!
How lifeless his glance!
Still—his heart!
No fleeting flutter
of his breath?
Must she stand mourning
by your side
who, so joyous, came here to wed you,
bravely sailing the sea?
Too late!
Obstinate man!
Why must my punishment
be so hard?
Is there no grace
for my sorrow's debt?
May I not tell you
what my complaints are?
Just once more, ah!
Just one more time!
Tristan! Ha!
Hark! He wakes!
Beloved!
(She sinks down senseless upon his body.)

Dritter Auftritt

Die Vorigen. Der Hirt. Der Steuermann. Melot. Brangäne.
Marke. Ritter und Knappen.

HIRT *(hastig und leise sich zu Kurwenal wendend)*:
> Kurwenal! Hör!
> Ein zweites Schiff.
> *(Kurwenal fährt heftig auf und blickt über*
> *die Brüstung, während der Hirt aus der*
> *Ferne erschüttert auf Tristan und Isolde*
> *sieht.)*

KURWENAL *(in Wut ausbrechend)*:
> Tod und Hölle!
> Alles zur Hand!
> Marke und Melot
> hab' ich erkannt.
> Waffen und Steine!
> Hilf mir! Ans Tor!
> *(Er eilt mit dem Hirten an das Tor, das sie*
> *in der Hast zu verrammeln suchen.)*

DER STEUERMANN *(stürzt herein)*:
> Marke mir nach
> mit Mann und Volk:
> vergebne Wehr!
> Bewältigt sind wir.

KURWENAL:
> Stell dich und hilf!
> Solang ich lebe,
> lugt mir keiner herein!

BRANGÄNES STIMME *(außen, von unten her)*:
> Isolde! Herrin!

Scene III

Kurvenal had entered immediately after Isolde; in speechless horror, he has remained near the entrance, gazing motionless on Tristan. From below is now heard the dull tumult of voices and clash of weapons. The shepherd climbs over the wall, then comes quickly and softly to Kurvenal.

SHEPHERD: Kurvenal! Hear!
              A second ship!

              Kurvenal starts up in haste and looks over the rampart, while the shepherd stands apart, gazing in consternation on Tristan and Isolde.

KURVENAL: Death and hell-fire!
              All of you, now!
              Melot and Mark
              I think I have seen!
              Weapons and stones too!
              Help me! To the gate!

              He hurries with the shepherd to the gate, which they hastily try to barricade.

THE STEERSMAN *(rushes in)*:
              Mark is behind
              with men-at-arms:
              defense is vain,
              we're overpowered.

KURVENAL: Stand here and help!
              While I am living
              none can pry into here!

BRANGAENE *(without, calling from below)*:
              Isolde! Mistress!

KURWENAL: Brangänens Ruf?
(Hinabrufend.)
Was suchst du hier?

BRANGÄNE: Schließ nicht, Kurwenal!
Wo ist Isolde?

KURWENAL: Verrät'rin auch du?
Weh dir, Verruchte!

MELOT *(außerhalb)*:
Zurück, du Tor!
Stemm dich nicht dort!

KURWENAL *(wütend auflachend)*:
Heiahaha! Dem Tag,
an dem ich dich treffe!
*(Melot, mit gewaffneten Männern, erscheint
unter dem Tor, Kurwenal stürzt sich auf
ihn und streckt ihn zu Boden.)*

KURWENAL: Stirb, schändlicher Wicht!

MELOT: Weh mir, Tristan! *(Er stirbt.)*

BRANGÄNE *(noch außerhalb)*:
Kurwenal! Wütender!
Hör, du betrügst dich!

KURWENAL: Treulose Magd!
(Zu den Seinen.)
Drauf! Mir nach!
Werft sie zurück!
(Sie kämpfen.)

MARKE *(außerhalb)*:
Halte, Rasender!
Bist du von Sinnen?

KURWENAL: Hier wütet der Tod!
Nichts andres, König,
ist hier zu holen:
willst du ihn kiesen, so komm!
*(Er dringt auf Marke und dessen Gefolge
ein.)*

KURVENAL: Brangaene's voice!
(Calling down.)
What do you seek?

BRANGAENE: Don't close, Kurvenal!
Where is Isolde?

KURVENAL: A traitor, you too?
Woe to you, rascal!

MELOT *(without)*:
Stand back, you fool!
Bar not the way!

KURVENAL *(laughing savagely)*:
Hi-a-ha-ha! The day
has come I can strike you!

Melot with armed men appears under the gateway. Kurvenal rushes upon him and strikes him down.

Die, villainous wretch!

MELOT: Woe's me! Tristan!
(He dies.)

BRANGAENE *(still without)*:
Kurvenal! Do not
deceive yourself, madman!

KURVENAL: Treacherous maid!
(To his followers.)
Come! Follow!
Hurl them right back!

They fight.

MARK *(half in)*: Halt, you blusterer!
Are you demented?

KURVENAL: Here rages but death!
There's nothing, King,
besides to be had here:
if you would choose it, then come!
(He sets upon Mark and his followers.)

MARKE *(unter dem Tor mit Gefolge erscheinend)*:
                    Zurück! Wahnsinniger!

BRANGÄNE *(hat sich seitwärts über die Mauer geschwungen
      und eilt in den Vordergrund)*:
                    Isolde! Herrin!
                    Glück und Heil!
                    Was seh' ich? Ha!
                    Lebst du? Isolde!
                    *(Sie müht sich um Isolde. — Marke mit
                    seinem Gefolge hat Kurwenal mit dessen
                    Helfern vom Tore zurückgetrieben und
                    dringt herein.)*

MARKE: O Trug und Wahn!
                    Tristan! Wo bist du?

KURWENAL *(schwer verwundet, schwankt vor Marke her nach
      dem Vordergrund)*:
                    Da liegt er —
                    hier — wo ich — liege.
                    (Er sinkt bei Tristans Füßen zusammen.)

MARKE: Tristan! Tristan!
                    Isolde! Weh!

KURWENAL *(nach Tristans Hand fassend)*:
                    Tristan! Trauter!
                    Schilt mich nicht,
                    daß der Treue auch mit kommt! *(Er stirbt.)*

MARKE: Tot denn alles!
                    Alles tot!
                    Mein Held, mein Tristan!
                    Trautester Freund,
                    auch heute noch
                    mußt du den Freund verraten?
                    Heut, wo er kommt,
                    dir höchste Treu' zu bewähren?
                    Erwache! Erwache!
                    Erwache meinem Jammer!
                    *(Schluchzend über die Leiche sich herab-
                    beugend.)*
                    Du treulos treuster Freund!

MARK (*appearing under the gate with his men*):
Go back, you maniac!

> *Brangaene has climbed over the wall at the side and hastens to the front.*

BRANGAENE:
Isolde! Mistress!
Joyful news!
(*Seeing her mistress senseless on the ground.*)
What sight's this? Ha!
(*She devotes herself to Isolde.*)
Are you still living?

MARK (*who with his followers has driven Kurvenal and his assistants back from the gate and forced his way in*):
Oh, dread mistake!
Tristan! Where are you?

> *Kurvenal, mortally wounded, totters before Mark toward the front.*

KURVENAL:
There lies he—
here—where I—lie too!
(*He sinks down at Tristan's feet.*)

MARK:
Tristan! Tristan!
Isolde! Woe!

KURVENAL (*clutching at Tristan's hand*):
Tristan! Master!
Blame me not
who, all faithful, join you now!
(*He dies.*)

MARK:
All are dead, then!
All are dead!
My hero, Tristan!
Truest of friends,
so even on
this day you must betray me?
Just when he comes
to prove his perfect trust in Tristan?
Awaken! Awaken!
Awaken to my sorrow!
(*Bending down sobbing over the bodies.*)
You faithless, faithful friend!

BRANGÄNE *(die in ihren Armen Isolde wieder zu sich gebracht)*:
Sie wacht! Sie lebt!
Isolde! Hör mich,
vernimm meine Sühne!
Des Trankes Geheimnis
entdeckt' ich dem König:
mit sorgender Eil'
stach er in See,
dich zu erreichen,
dir zu entsagen,
dir zuzuführen den Freund.

MARKE:
Warum, Isolde,
warum mir das?
Da hell mir enthüllt,
was zuvor ich nicht fassen konnt',
wie selig, daß den Freund
ich frei von Schuld da fand!
Dem holden Mann
dich zu vermählen,
mit vollen Segeln
flog ich dir nach.
Doch Unglückes
Ungestüm,
wie erreicht es, wer Frieden bringt?
Die Ernte mehrt' ich dem Tod,
der Wahn häufte die Not.

BRANGÄNE:
Hörst du uns nicht?
Isolde! Traute!
Vernimmst du die Treue nicht?
*(Isolde, die nichts um sich her vernommen,
heftet das Auge mit wachsender Begeister-
ung auf Tristans Leiche.)*

ISOLDE:
Mild und leise
wie er lächelt,
wie das Auge
hold er öffnet —
seht ihr's, Freunde?
Seht ihr's nicht?
Immer lichter
wie er leuchtet,

BRANGAENE *(who has revived Isolde in her arms)*:

> She wakes! She lives!
> Isolde, hear me!
> Oh, hear my atonement!
> The king knows the secret:
> I told of the potion.
> He sped over sea,
> greatly concerned
> that he might reach you,
> just to renounce you
> and make you one with your friend!

MARK:

> Oh, why, Isolde,
> why this to me?
> When that was revealed
> which before I had failed to grasp,
> how blessed that I found
> my friend was free from guilt!
> That you might wed
> hero so gallant,
> with outspread sails
> I flew in your wake.
> Yet how can one bringing peace
> get the better of raging woe!
> I swelled the harvest of death;
> Vain dreams only heap woe!

BRANGAENE:

> Do you not hear?
> Isolde! Dearest!
> Oh, look on your faithful maid!

ISOLDE *(unconscious of all around her, turning her eyes on Tristan's body with rising inspiration)*:

> See him smiling,
> softly, gently,
> see the eyes that
> open fondly,
> O my friends here,
> don't you see?
> Ever lighter
> how he's shining,

stern-umstrahlet
hoch sich hebt?
Seht ihr's nicht?
Wie das Herz ihm
mutig schwillt,
voll und hehr
im Busen ihm quillt?
Wie den Lippen,
wonnig mild,
süßer Atem
sanft entweht —
Freunde! Seht!
Fühlt und seht ihr's nicht?
Hör' ich nur
diese Weise,
die so wunder-
voll und leise,
Wonne klagend,
alles sagend,
mild versöhnend
aus ihm tönend,
in mich dringet,
auf sich schwinget,
hold erhallend
um mich klinget?
Heller schallend,
mich umwallend,
sind es Wellen
sanfter Lüfte?
Sind es Wogen
wonniger Düfte?
Wie sie schwellen,
mich umrauschen,
soll ich atmen,
soll ich lauschen?
Soll ich schlürfen,
untertauchen?
Süß in Düften
mich verhauchen?
In dem wogenden Schwall,
in dem tönenden Schall,

borne on high
amid the stars?
Don't you see?
How his heart so
bravely swells,
full and calm
it throbs in his breast!
How from lips so
joyful-mild
sweet the breath that
softly stirs—
Friends! See!
Don't you feel and see?
Is it only
I who hear these
gentle, wondrous
strains of music,
joyously sounding,
telling all things,
reconciling,
sounding from him,
piercing through me,
rising upward,
echoes fondly
round me ringing?
Ever clearer,
wafting round me,
are they waves of
gentle breezes?
Are they clouds of
gladdening perfumes?
As they swell and
murmur round me,
shall I breathe them,
shall I listen?
Shall I sip them,
plunge beneath them,
breathe my last
amid their fragrance?
In the billowy surge,
in the ocean of sound,

in des Welt-Atems
wehendem All —
ertrinken,
versinken —
unbewußt —
höchste Lust!
(Isolde sinkt, wie verklärt, in Brangänes
Armen sanft auf Tristans Leiche. Große
Rührung und Entrücktheit unter den Umste-
henden. Marke segnet die Leichen. Der Vor-
hang fällt langsam.)

in the World Spirit's
infinite All,
to drown now,
descending,
void of thought—
highest bliss!

*Isolde sinks, as if transfigured, in Brangaene's
arms upon Tristan's body. Profound emotion
and grief of the bystanders. Mark invokes a
blessing on the dead.*

CURTAIN

DATE DUE